STATE PARKS OF THE WEST : AMER
F 595.3 D42 1990

DATE DUE

'97			

STATE PARKS OF THE WEST

STATE PARKS OF THE WEST

America's Best-Kept Secrets

A Guide to
Camping, Fishing, Hiking,
& Sightseeing

Vici DeHaan

CORDILLERA PRESS, INC.

Publishers in the Rockies

Library of Congress Cataloging-in-Publication Data
DeHaan, Vici.
    State parks of the West : America's best-kept secrets : a guide to camping, fishing, hiking & sightseeing / Vici DeHaan.
        p.   cm.
    ISBN 0-917895-31-2 : $13.95
    1. Parks — West (U.S.) — Guide-books.   2. West (U.S.) — Description and travel — 1981- — Guide-books.   3. Outdoor recreation — West (U.S.) — Guide-books.   I. Title.
    F595.3.D42   1989
    917.804'33 — dc20   89-77671
                                                                              CIP

First Edition
    2   3   4   5   6   7   8   9

Printed in the United States of America.

Front Cover Photograph
    Redwood giants along California's northern coast. ERIC J. WUNROW
Back Cover Photographs
    Hawaii welcome and California coast. VICI DEHAAN
    Oregon lighthouse, Nevada desert, and Arizona cactus. ERIC J. WUNROW

Cover Design & Typography
    Richard M. Kohen / *Shadow Canyon Graphics*
Interior Design & Typography
    Richard M. Kohen / *Shadow Canyon Graphics* · *Evergreen, Colorado*

Cordillera Press, Inc.
Post Office Box 3699
Evergreen, Colorado 80439
(303) 670-3010

Contents

IDAHO 97

MONTANA 111

NEVADA 121

WASHINGTON 185

WYOMING 209

State Park Index and a Summary of Park Features 219

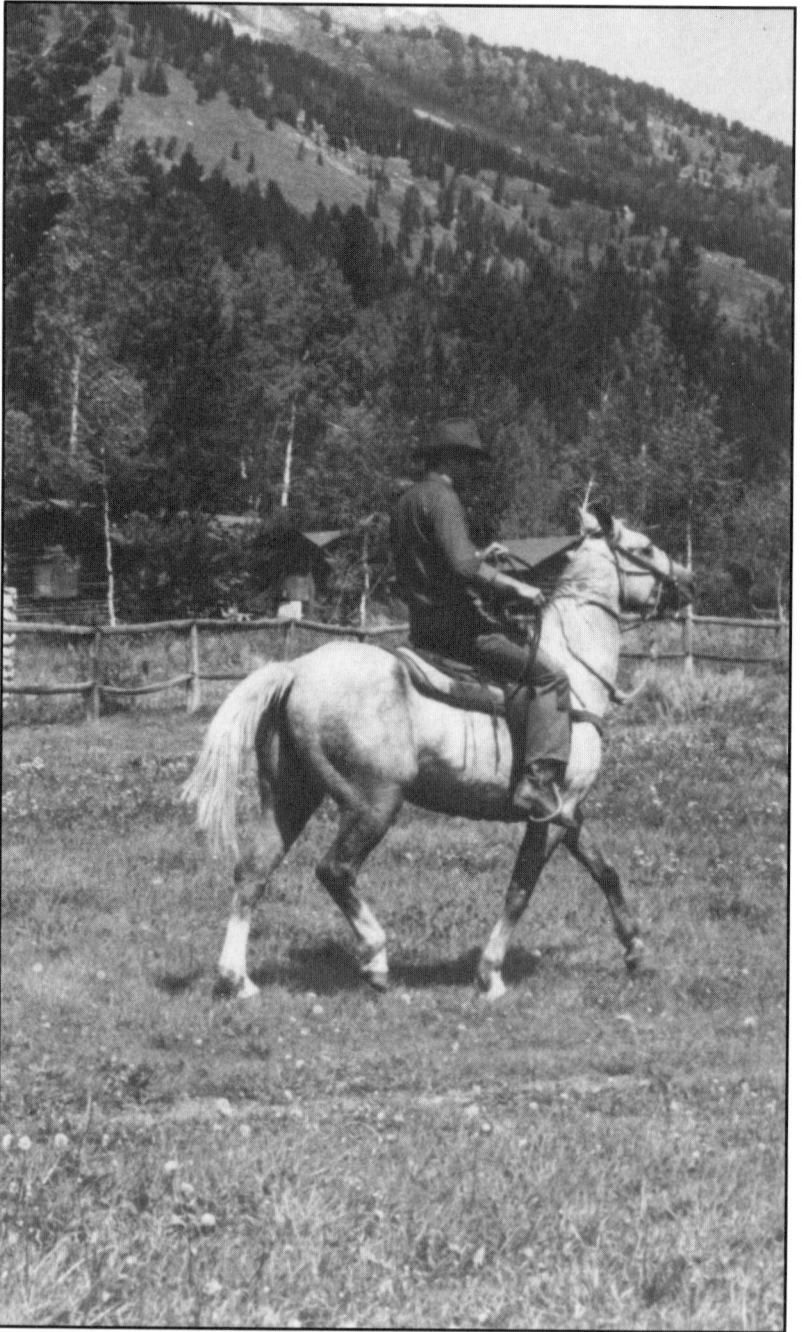

Hitting the trail.
WYOMING TRAVEL COMMISSION

AMERICA'S
Best-Kept Secrets

Have you ever wondered what you might be missing by only visiting our national parks and major attractions? What secrets and special places await discovery nearby? My fascination with traveling and discovering new places has been in my blood ever since I was a small child. During World War II, my parents drove our family from Colorado to Massachusetts on many summer trips to see my paternal grandparents. We hardly ever took the same route twice, and thus my life-long love affair with the open road began.

Now that I am an adult and can travel to places of my own choosing, I have had a wonderful time exploring this fantastic country of ours. Among my most interesting discoveries have been the state parks of the western United States. In many instances, their stunning beauty, special events, and frequently fewer crowds make them America's best-kept secrets.

State Parks of the West shares with you the secrets of almost 300 state parks throughout Alaska, Arizona, California, Colorado, Hawaii, Idaho, Montana, Nevada, New Mexico, Oregon, Utah, Washington, and Wyoming. The parks included in this guide are not meant to be a comprehensive listing of every park in each state — there are simply too many and some are very small parks located along a beach or reservoir. Instead, I have included a wide and varied selection from each state so that the traveler unfamiliar with the area will get a good idea of what possibilities await.

The section on each park includes location and directions, interesting features, activities and facilities, and addresses and telephone numbers. I've included hours and seasons of operations in some cases, but please, please, remember that these are subject to change. If this guide says the ferry runs at 2:00 p.m., you would be well advised to check a current time schedule and confirm that information. Other major information includes camping facilities, hiking trails, fishing tips, swimming and boating activities, interpretive programs, and nearby attractions.

My husband and I are private pilots and there is information on airfields and nearby accommodations. We found that the state parks are great places to exercise and keep in shape, so included are suggestions for bicyclists about tours and trails and notes for runners and triathletes on competitions and training locations.

Some of our favorite experiences have been with the special events we have encountered in or near the state parks we've visited — whether it was a kite flying festival at Yaquina Bay State Park in Oregon, a rodeo in Great Falls, Montana, or a Civil War reenactment in Arizona. Again, be sure to double-check local schedules and information.

I hope my experiences and research help make your own travels even more rewarding. Keep this guide in your auto, RV, airplane, or boat, and when the call of the open road strikes, you won't be at a loss for new and interesting places to explore.

Collier Memorial State Park in Oregon boasts a fine logging museum.

Totem pole in Sitka.
VICI DEHAAN

ALASKA

One of the nicest features of visiting Alaska, along with its spectacular scenery, is the 18-22 hours of daylight you have for exploring during the summer months.

If you decide to venture out fishing or camping in the backcountry with a bush pilot, be prepared to stay in your location longer than you planned. Weather is unpredictable, and your pilot may not be able to pick you up when promised.

Bears are one of the main attractions in Alaska, but they can be quite unpredictable and dangerous if you're not careful. It's imperative that you keep a clean campsite and remove all odors of cooking from your clothing and hands. Don't keep any food in your tent. Store all garbage in the containers provided or pack it out.

If you're hiking in bear country, carry something to make noise — such as a can with stones that you can rattle, wear a bell, or talk loudly. If you give the resident bears a chance to leave the area you're hiking in, they probably will. If you're hiking in dense bush, in the wind, or near any running water, however, you may not be heard. If possible, keep your back to the wind. The last thing you want to do is surprise a bear, for as the saying goes, "Don't surprise one or you might likewise be surprised."

Watch where you camp when in the backcountry. Avoid camping on bear trails, most commonly found along salmon streams, near berry patches, or in saddles along the ridgetops. Pick your campsites downwind from their trails, which you can identify by watching for any oval-shaped depressions in the trail. Bears often step in the same places as they walk.

Bears may make a wolfing sound as they turn to run, which is what you hope will happen. But, if one decides to stand its ground and begins making a series of woofs, pops its teeth, or turns sideways, seeming to be looking off into the distance, it's time for you to leave the area slowly, always facing the bear.

If you are faced with a true encounter, and if it's a grizzly, speak softly to it and try to back over to a tree which you can climb. Grizzlies don't usually

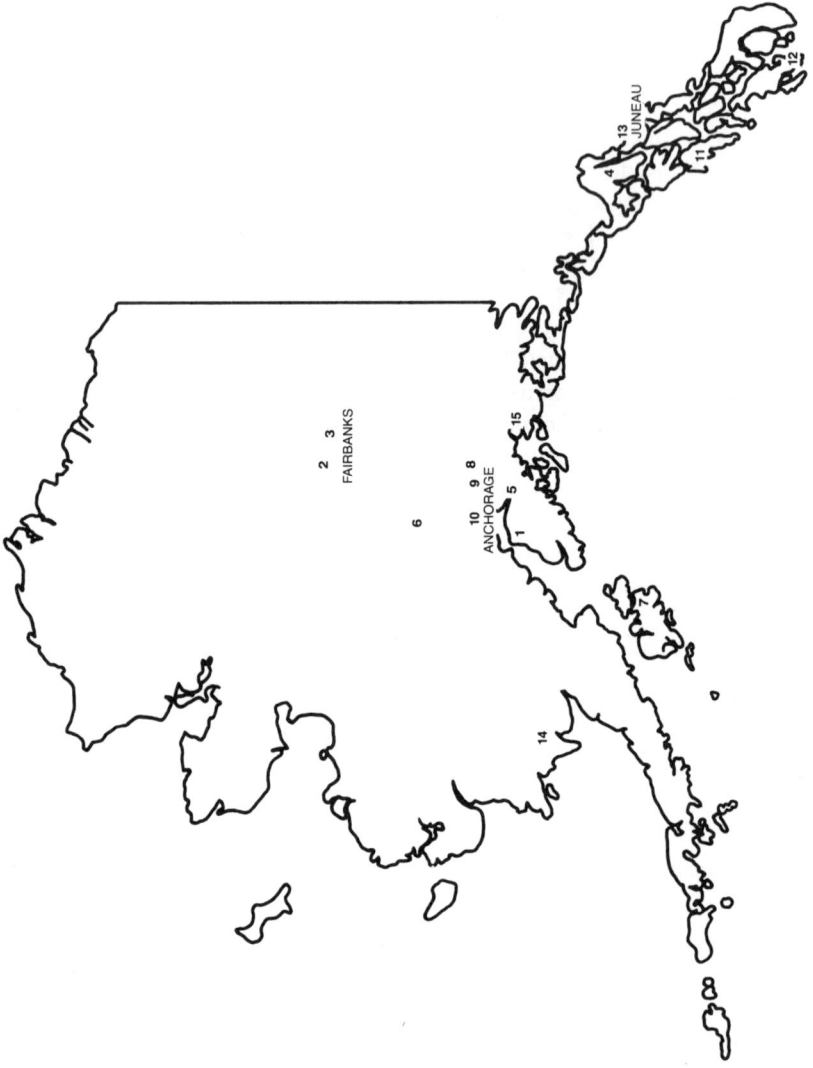

FAIRBANKS

JUNEAU

ANCHORAGE

2 3

4

6

5

8 9 10

11

12

13

14

15

climb trees. On the other hand, if it's a black bear, don't even think about climbing, because they are very good tree climbers.

If the bear decides to follow you as you slowly attempt to vacate the area, drop some clothing for it to smell. If all else fails and you are actually attacked, play dead. Lie face down, pull your legs up to your chest, and clasp your hands over the back of your neck. If you're wearing a backpack, keep it on to protect your back.

Mosquitoes in Alaska can be very ferocious. It's no wonder they're often referred to as "Alaska's state bird." Be sure to bring along plenty of repellent and wear long-sleeved shirts.

Assume that the backcountry water has been infected with giardia, and boil or treat your drinking water with purification tablets.

If you're exploring the tidal flats near Anchorage, be wary of the bore tides that can come rushing in at 20 m.p.h.

Boaters should be prepared to carry the necessary equipment to prevent hypothermia should you end up in the extremely cold water. If you do capsize, be sure to stay with the boat rather than trying to swim to shore.

Before you strike out into the backcountry, leave an itinerary with the local rangers so they know when you expect to return. As you take the time to do this, you can also obtain the latest information to make your foray more successful.

For additional information on Alaska state parks:
Alaska State Park Information
Box 107001-TP
Anchorage, Alaska 99510

CAPTAIN COOK STATE RECREATION AREA
1

LOCATION - Thirty miles north of Kenai on the North Kenai Road.

FEATURES - The area has 3,500 acres of saltwater beaches, forests, lakes and rivers.

ACTIVITIES - Camp in one of the drive-in or more remote campgrounds. Picnic on the bluff overlooking the Cook Inlet. Go hiking, fishing or boating from the small boat launch. You can also go swimming from the beach.

INFORMATION -
Captain Cook State Recreation Area
Box 1247-TP
Soldotna, Alaska 99669
907-262-5581

CHATANIKA RIVER STATE RECREATION SITE AND RECREATION AREA
2

LOCATION - Upper Chatanika River is northwest of Fairbanks off Alaska 6 at 39 Steese. Lower Chatanika River is at Milepost 9 at 11 Elliott off Alaska 2.

ACTIVITIES - On the upper part of the river, you can fish and camp in their campground with 25 sites. On the lower part of the river, you can go fishing, boating and camping in one of 15 campsites in Whitefish Campground in the state recreation site, or in one of 50 sites found in Olnes Pond in the state recreation area.

INFORMATION -
Chatanika River State Recreation Site and Recreation Area
Northern Region Park Office
4418 Airport Way
Fairbanks, Alaska 99701
907-479-4114

CHENA RIVER STATE RECREATION AREA
3

LOCATION - On the Chena Hot Springs Road, an hour's drive northeast of Fairbanks.

ACTIVITIES - Go fishing, boating or canoeing on the Chena River. The park has two campgrounds. Rosehip has 38 sites and Tors Trail has 18 sites. Cabins are available near Fairbanks. To rent one of the cabins, contact the Northern Region Park office at 4418 Airport Way, Fairbanks, 99701, 907-479-4114.

Hike to the prominent granite formations where you can observe bear, beaver and moose. Lower and Upper Chena Dome Trailheads are located at Milepost 49 and 50.5 on the Chena Hot Springs Road.

While in Chena, take a cruise on the Chena and Tanana rivers aboard an authentic sternwheeler. In July, attend the World Eskimo-Indian Olympics where traditional dances and athletic competitions are featured.

INFORMATION -
Chena River State Recreation Area
4418-TP
Airport Way

Fairbanks, Alaska 99701
907-479-4114

CHILKAT STATE PARK
4

LOCATION - South of Haines on the Chilkat peninsula at 7 Mud Bay Road.

ACTIVITIES - Visitors can get some fantastic views of the glaciers across the Chilkat Inlet. Watch for whales, seals and other wildlife.

Go camping in one of 32 sites where you have a good look at the glaciers from your tent, have a picnic, go boating and fishing from the ramp, or hike the trails.

Visit nearby Port Chilkoot where you can watch the well-known Chilkat Indian dancers perform on Monday, Wednesday and Saturday at 8:30 during the summer months.

Attend a performance of "Lust for Dust" on Friday or Sunday. For information, call 907-766-2540.

Take a four-hour raft trip through Chilkat Bald Eagle Preserve. For information: Box 170-TP, Haines, Alaska, 99827; 907-766-2409.

If you're in the area between October and January, drive the Haines Highway to the Chilkat Bald Eagle Preserve where approximately 3,500 bald eagles congregate.

INFORMATION -
Chilkat State Park
Box 518-TP
Haines, Alaska 99827
907-766-2234 or 766-2202

CHUGACH STATE PARK
5

LOCATION - The park is 45 miles south of Anchorage on the Glenn Highway.

ACTIVITIES - Observe the wildlife. Go camping, hiking and mountain climbing.

Tour the Eagle River Visitor Center at Milepost 12 on the Eagle River Road and the Potter Section House Historic Site at 115 Seward Highway to see an interpretive program.

The Eklutna Campground is near Palmer at Milepost 26.5 on the Glenn

Highway and has 50 campsites, picnicking facilities, hiking trails and fishing. The Eagle River Campground also has 50 sites and is located at Milepost 12.6 on the Glenn Highway. At the Williwaw Campground, you can watch salmon during their spawning season.

The park has several trail systems and information may be picked up at the visitor center.

INFORMATION -
Chugach State Park
201-TP East Fourth Avenue
Anchorage, Alaska 99501
907-271-2500

DENALI STATE PARK
6

LOCATION - 130 miles north of Anchorage. Access into the park is available year-round from either Fairbanks or Anchorage on Alaska 3, and on Alaska 8 from Paxson from early June to mid-October. You can also ride the Alaska Railroad which offers daily service between Fairbanks and Anchorage from late May to mid-September. For quicker entry, check out the possibility of taking a charter flight from an airport in either Anchorage or Fairbanks.

FEATURES - Denali means "The Great One" in Tanaina Indian dialect. This majestic mountain is one of the park's main attractions.

The largest northward-flowing glacier to be found in Alaska, the Muldrow, is located on Mount McKinley's northern slopes and may be seen from the road on a clear day. The mountain itself is shrouded in clouds 75 percent of the time during the summer, however, and 60 percent of the time the rest of the year, so hope for one of those rare days.

ACTIVITIES - Most visitors can drive only the first 12 miles into the park. After that point, only those holding assigned campsite permits are allowed to continue on. Campers may elect to hop a shuttle bus to reach their campsites. Campsites are available at Denali, Riley Creek, Savage River, Sanctuary River, Teklanika River, Igloo Creek and at Wonder Lake, where 20 tent sites are available.

To register for a campsite, contact the Riley Creek Information Center. Anyone planning to drive into the park should be sure to leave with a full tank of gas since no gas or supplies are available within the park. You're also advised to purchase any food you need for camping either in Fairbanks or Anchorage so you won't be faced with higher food prices as you get closer to the park.

If you're planning to tour the area, you can board one of the shuttles that run into the park from the hotel. These shuttles may be taken to the Eielson Visitor Center, to Wonder Lake 84 miles away, or you may arrange to be dropped off anywhere along the road you choose. When you're ready to return, you simply board the next bus that comes along.

Park rangers give interpretive talks at the campgrounds. For information on these and other park activities, stop by the various ranger stations, the Eielson Visitor Center, or the Denali Park Station Hotel.

Camp Denali is located two miles north of Wonder Lake and offers sourdough vacations. If you're interested, write to Camp Denali, P.O. Box 67, Denali National Park, Alaska 99755, or call 907-683-2302 during the winter, or 907-683-2290 during the summer. The camp operates from early June through early September.

Hike the trails to Curry Ridge. Trails are at Little Coal Creek, Milepost 163.9 Parks Road; Upper or Lower Troublesome Creek Trailheads at Milepost 137.6 and 137.2 Parks Road, and Denali Viewpoint at Milepost 135.2 Parks Road.

Take a discovery hike with the park service. One hike goes to the end of the Muldrow Glacier while another hike climbs up 1,500 feet to Primrose Ridge.

Tundra Wildlife Tours operates daily from the McKinley Park Station Hotel. For information call 907-278-1122.

If you're up for a horseback or mule ride, contact Alaska Range Wilderness at 907-683-2525.

Seven miles south of the park entrance at McKinley Village, you can arrange to take a river float trip down the Nenana River. Daytime trips last for two and one-half hours, and evening tours go for two hours. For information, call 907-683-2234.

Fishing is reported to be quite poor within the park, but is better in the clear water streams. Try to avoid any streams with glacial silt which makes the water appear to be quite milky.

For the best view of Mount McKinley, however, you can't beat seeing it from the air. If you luck out on the weather, and can either fly yourself by checking out in a light plane from one of the airports or locate a charter flight, you'll be in for a trip you'll never forget. When the weather does clear, however, everyone who owns a plane will probably be out flying and finding a rental plane may not be very easy. It took us an hour of calling every flight station in the area before we managed to find one, but it was well worth the time and effort.

INFORMATION -
Superintendent
Denali National Park
P.O. Box 9

McKinley Park, Alaska 99755
907-683-2294
or
Denali State Park
SOA-Division Parks/ODR
Box 6706-TP
Wasilla, Alaska 99687-9717
907-745-3975

FORT AMBERCROMBIE STATE HISTORIC PARK
7

LOCATION - Northeast of Kodiak on Kodiak Island, southwest of Anchorage. To reach Kodiak, you can either fly from Anchorage or Seattle, or take a ferry from Homer, Seldovia or from Seward.

FEATURES - Kodiak Island is famous for its Kodiak or Alaskan brown bears and is a favorite spot for hunters. You can hire guides and outfitters for your hunting expedition in Kodiak.

ACTIVITIES - Explore the remains of the artillery fort which commemorates Alaska's role in World War II. Tour the ranger station.

Camp in the campground or enjoy a picnic near the fresh water lake. Hike through the meadows or among the Sitka spruce. Free cabins are available in the Kodiak National Wildlife Refuge. For information, phone 907-487-2600, or write the Refuge Manager at Kodiak National Wildlife Refuge, Box 825, Kodiak, 99615.

In Kodiak, in August, attend their outdoor pageant, "Cry of the Wild Ram." The play commemorates the residents' Russian heritage since the town was the capital of Russian Americans from 1783 until 1799. In May, attend the Kodiak Crab Festival. For information, call 907-486-5291 or write Box 1792-TP, Kodiak, Alaska, 99615.

You can also tour the Russian Orthodox Church and the Baranof Museum housed in a historic fur storehouse on the waterfront which is Alaska's oldest wooden structure. Information for the museum may be obtained by calling 907-486-5920.

INFORMATION -
Fort Ambercrombie State Historic Park
Box 3800-TP
Kodiak, Alaska 99801
907-486-6339

INDEPENDENCE MINE STATE HISTORIC PARK
8

LOCATION - In the Talkeetna Mountains, a two hour drive from Anchorage.

FEATURES - The park has some abandoned buildings and machinery left behind in the camp where 200 hardrock miners searched for gold during the 1940s.

ACTIVITIES - Part of the beauty of visiting this park is the drive over Hatcher Pass, particularly if you take the 50-mile loop drive between George Parks and Glenn highways.

Tour the mine manager's house and other buildings to see some interpretive displays. You can take a walking tour of the camp to see the equipment used in the two gold mines. Guided tours are offered during their season from late May through late September.

INFORMATION -
Independence Mine State Historic Park
SOA-Division Parks/ODR
SR Box 6706-TP
Wasilla, Alaska 99687-9719
907-743-3975

KEPLER-BRADLEY LAKES STATE RECREATION AREA
9

LOCATION - Near Palmer northeast of Anchorage

ACTIVITIES - The area has four lakes: Matanuska, Canoe, Irene and Long Lakes where you have a choice of 344 campsites and plenty of fishing opportunities.

The Matanuska Valley is famous for its 70-pound cabbages. Visitors are invited to tour the Matanuska Agricultural Experimental Farm seven miles southwest of Palmer to see some of these very large vegetables.

INFORMATION -
Kepler-Bradley Lakes State Recreation Area
Palmer Chamber of Commerce
Box 45-TP
Palmer, Alaska 99645
907-745-2880

NANCY LAKE STATE RECREATION AREA
10

LOCATION - The area is south of Willow on Parks Highway at Mile 67.

ACTIVITIES - Go canoeing, fishing or boating on over 130 lakes. Camp in the campgrounds or go hiking. The area has a system of canoe portages. You can also rent one of the four public rental cabins. For information, contact the regional park office: Matanuska-Susitna/Copper Basin Area Office, SR Box 6706, Wasilla, Alaska, 99687, 907-745-3975.

Trailheads are located at Milepost 1.8 Nancy Lake Parkway, Tulik Trailhead at Milepost 3.5 Nancy Lake Parkway, and the Canoe System Trailhead is at Milepost 4.8 Nancy Lake Parkway. The South Rolly Lake Campground is at Milepost 6.5 Nancy Lake Parkway and has 98 campsites.

Nancy Lake State Recreation Site is at Milepost 66.5 Parks Road and has 36 campsites, boating and fishing.

INFORMATION -
Nancy Lake State Recreation Area
SOA Division Parks/ODR
SR Box 6706-TP
Wasilla, Alaska 99687-9719
907-745-3975

SITKA STATE PARKS
11

REFUGE COVE
SITKA STATE PARKS

Refuge Cove is located at 8.7 North Tongass Road where you can have a picnic and go fishing.

SETTLERS COVE
SITKA STATE PARKS

Settlers Cove is located at 18 North Tongass Road where you can enjoy hiking, fishing or camp in one of 12 sites.

PIONEER PARK
SITKA STATE PARKS

Pioneer Park is located at 2 Habitat Road where you can go hiking.

BARANOF CASTLE STATE HISTORIC SITE
SITKA STATE PARKS

Baranof Castle State Historic Site is located on Lincoln Street where you can tour the castle.

INFORMATION -
Sitka Convention and Visitors Bureau
Department W. 330 Harbor Drive
Sitka, Alaska 99840
907-747-5940

TOTEM BIGHT STATE HISTORIC PARK
12

LOCATION - Ten miles north of Ketchikan on North Tongass Highway at 10 Tongass Road.

FEATURES - The park is dedicated to Southeast Alaska's native cultures and features a dozen totem poles plus a tribal lodgehouse.

ACTIVITIES - Hike along an interpretive trail through the rain forest to the clan house. Get a good look at the Tlingit and Haida totem poles. It's also a great place to see the Tongass Narrows.

You can see additional totem poles in the Saxman Totem Park located 2.5 miles south on the South Tongass Highway.

For an even larger collection of totem poles, visit Sitka National Historical Park located a mile east of town. This area has 28 poles, some dating back over 100 years.

INFORMATION -
Totem Bight State Historic Park
Box M-D-TP
Alaska Division of Parks
Juneau, Alaska 99811
907-465-4563

WICKERSHAM STATE HISTORIC SITE
13

LOCATION - 213 7th Street in Juneau.

ACTIVITIES - Take a guided tour through the former residence of Judge James Wickersham who was a well-known historian, pioneer judge and statesman. Visitors can see Russian and pioneer artifacts and original furnishings. As part of the tour, you'll be served flaming sourdough. Make your reservations for either 1:30 or 6:30 from late May through the first of October. Call 907-586-1251.

From Juneau, drive 13 miles northwest of town on Alaska 7 on the Mendenhall Loop Road to see the Mendenhall Glacier. Hike up the nature trail to learn more about the glaciation in the area. Watch salmon as they return to spawn up Steep Creek either from mid-July through mid-August or from mid-September through early December. Tour the visitor center's observatory and attend an interpretive talk by one of the naturalists.

INFORMATION -
Wickersham State Historic Site
213 7th Street
Juneau, Alaska 99811
907-789-0097

WOOD-TIKCHIK STATE PARK
14

LOCATION - 300 air miles southwest from Anchorage. To reach the park, fly to Dillingham from Anchorage via a regularly scheduled airline, and then charter a floatplane from Dillingham.

FEATURES - This state park is Alaska's most remote park as well as being the largest state park in the United States.

ACTIVITIES - The park itself is undeveloped, but visitors can enjoy trophy fishing for salmon, trout, grayling and arctic char, and go boating or rafting on the Tikchik and Wood River Lakes. Stay in privately-owned lodges. Advance reservations are necessary.

INFORMATION -
Wood-Tikchik State Park
General Delivery-TP
Dillingham, Alaska 99510
907-842-2375 (summer)
907-694-2108 (winter)

WORTHINGTON GLACIER STATE RECREATION AREA
15

LOCATION - The glacier is 30 miles east of Valdez on Alaska 4. Milepost 28.7 gives the visitor the best vantage point of the glacier, considered to be Alaska's most accessible.

ACTIVITIES - Hike a short trail to get a close-up look at the blue glacial ice. The area is considered a photographer's paradise. You can even camp at the foot of the glacier. Tour the visitor center housed in a log cabin at Dry Creek State Recreation Site on the Richardson Highway at Milepost 117.5.

INFORMATION -
Worthington Glacier State Recreation Area
Box 107001-TP
Anchorage, Alaska 99510
907-762-2600

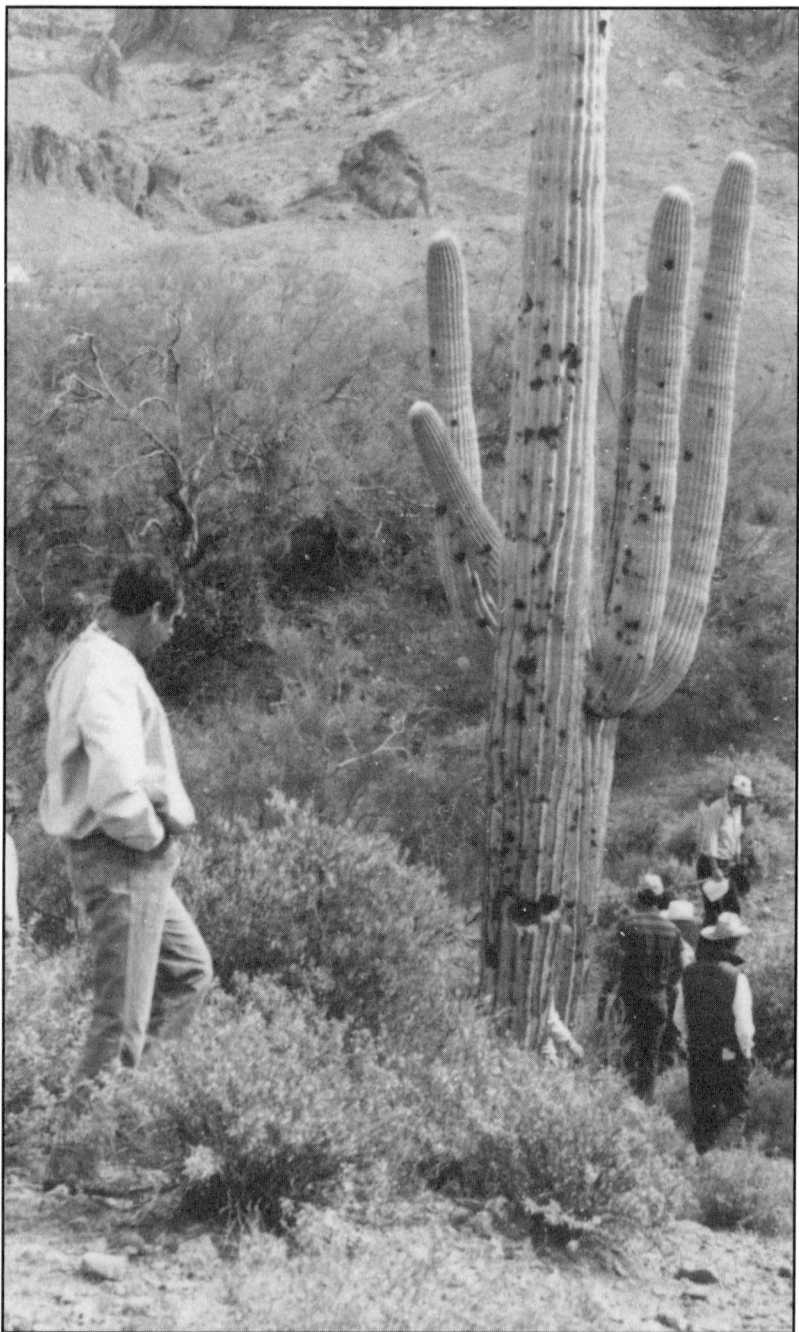

Lost Dutchman State Park.

WARREN DEHAAN

ARIZONA

Many people think of desert when they think about visiting Arizona, but you can also enjoy mountains, lakes and plateaus "painted" with rocks of many colors. Of course, the Grand Canyon is one of the state's most well-known sites, but if you get the chance to fly over the rock formations surrounding the canyon, you'll see some spectacular countryside.

For visitors who enjoy outdoor activities, it's a great place to visit either during the winter when the temperatures are truly delightful, or in the spring, especially when the desert has had enough rain to create a carpet of flowers.

ALAMO LAKE STATE PARK
1

LOCATION - On the Bill Williams River, 38 miles north of Wenden along an unmarked county road and 40 miles east of Lake Havasu. Access from Havasu is by boat along the river.

FEATURES - The lake covers the site of a mining camp called Alamo Crossing, which was established at the end of the nineteenth century as a supply store and post office for prospectors. For a few years, a small stamp mill processed gold and silver until the local mines stopped producing.

ACTIVITIES - Enjoy fishing for bass, catfish and bluegill. You can also camp year-round in your choice of undeveloped sites, developed sites, or ones with complete hookups. Enjoy a picnic, go sailing, boating water skiing, rockhounding or hiking. Because of the underwater hazards, swimming and scuba diving are not recommended.

The lake is open to waterfowl hunting in season. Watch for bald and golden eagles, fox, coyote, mule deer and wild burro.

Food service and concessions for boating and fishing are available.

INFORMATION -
Alamo Lake State Park

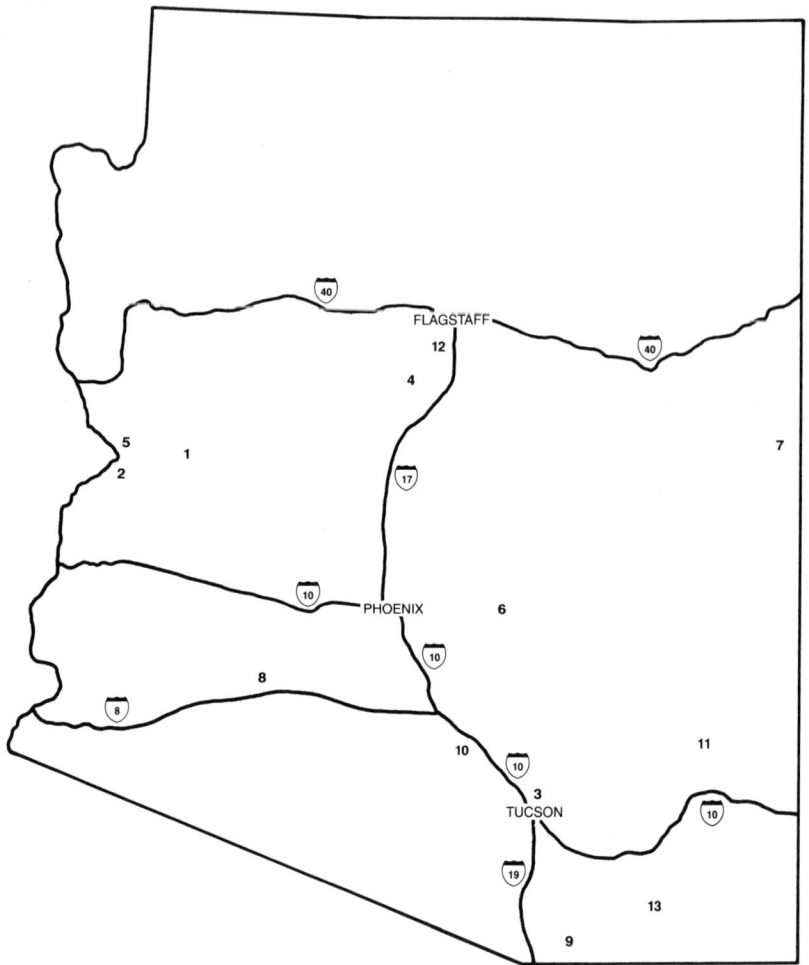

Box 38
Wenden, Arizona 85357
602-669-2088

BUCKSKIN MOUNTAIN STATE PARK
2

LOCATION - Eleven miles north of Parker on Arizona 95, near Parker Dam.

ACTIVITIES - The Colorado River runs beside the park where visitors can enjoy camping, picnicking, hiking, boating, fishing, swimming, a visitor center and food service. Three trails go into the Buckskin Range where you might be lucky enough to catch a glimpse of the desert bighorn sheep. Boat rentals are available, and campers are encouraged to arrive early in the day because of the campground's popularity.

Parker Dam and power plant is 12 miles northeast of town on Arizona 95. This is the world's deepest dam with 65% of its height lying below the riverbed. Take a free self-guided tour from 8-5.

INFORMATION -
Buckskin Mountain State Park
P.O. Box BA
Parker, Arizona 85344
602-667-3231

CATALINA STATE PARK
3

LOCATION - This desert park is located at the base of the northwestern slopes of the Catalina Mountains, nine miles north of Tucson on U.S. 89. It encompasses over 5,500 acres and is 4,000 feet above sea level.

ACTIVITIES - Go camping or enjoy a picnic in the park which has drinking water available. You can also go horseback riding, tour the visitor center, or hike nature trails. The Romero Canyon Trail passes both the Montrose Pools and the Romero Pools. Additional trails are located in adjacent Coronado National Forest.

You're also close to Saguaro National Monument, which has two sections. These giant saguaro cactus grow about two inches a year and take around 50 years before they put out an "arm." They bloom in April or May, but the flowers open nocturnally. They open around midnight and close by noon the following day. The Tucson Mountain section has rock formations decorated with Indian pictographs. Touring in this section is free. For information: 602-883-6366.

INFORMATION -
Catalina State Park
P.O. Box 36986
Tucson, Arizona 85740
602-628-5798

DEAD HORSE RANCH STATE PARK
4

LOCATION - The park is across the river to the north of Cottonwood. Enter on North 5th Street off U.S. 89A.

ACTIVITIES - The park is in one of the most scenic parts of Arizona. It's near the Tuzigoot National Monument which is two miles east of Clarkdale and was set aside to preserve the pueblo ruins of a Sinaguan village occupied from 1125 to 1400.

Camp in one of 45 sites operated on a first-come, first-served basis. Fish either in the Verde River or in the park lagoon which is usually stocked with panfish, catfish and bass. Trout are stocked here during the winter. An Arizona fishing license is required.

You can also go for a horseback ride, tour the visitor center or go for a hike. The park has access into the nearby national forest.

The drive down Oak Creek Canyon near Sedona is well known for its unforgettable scenery because of its many beautiful rock formations and gorges. Oak Creek is noted for its great trout fishing. Sedona is the jumping off point for jeeping and hiking in the Red Rocks area. For further information, contact the Sedona Chamber of Commerce: 602-282-7722.

INFORMATION -
Dead Horse Ranch State Park
Box 144
Cottonwood, Arizona 86326
602-634-5283

LAKE HAVASU STATE PARK
5

LOCATION - The park has three units located on the Colorado River near Lake Havasu City. Park headquarters is at Lake Havasu City across from the

London Bridge.

Lake Havasu is 46 miles long, but only three miles wide. It was formed when Parker Dam was built. You can cross the lake on paved roads located at both ends, one at Topock and the other at Parker Dam.

The average high temperature is 88 degrees, with an average low of 56 degrees. Generally, the climate is clear and dry.

ACTIVITIES - Lake Havasu has good fishing for bass, catfish and crappie. Water activities include boating, swimming, water and jet skiing.

Cattail Cove is 15 miles south of Lake Havasu City on Arizona 95. Activities include camping, with 150 of the sites accessible only by boat, picnicking, boating, fishing, swimming and a visitor center. The Sand Point Marina and Campground has a restaurant, camper supply store, boat rentals, repairs and special events. For information and reservations: 602-855-0540 or 855-0549. Headquarters: 602-855-1223

Pittsburgh Point is at Lake Havasu City on Arizona 95. Enjoy camping, picnicking, boating, fishing, swimming and touring the visitor center. A lodge, cabins and food service are available.

Windsor Beach is north of the London Bridge at the end of Crystal Avenue. The area offers picnicking, hiking, boating, fishing and swimming. You can also camp in rustic campsites along isolated coves accessible only by boats as well as in more developed campsites. To contact headquarters, call 602-855-2784.

Lake Havasu City is a year-round resort community situated by the London Bridge which was dismantled in London and shipped to Havasu where it was carefully reassembled. Many shops and restaurants surround the bridge, and you can take boat tours under it. Contact Lake Havasu Tours, Inc.: 602-855-7999.

Rockhounds hunt for agate, jasper, quartz, turquoise and Apache tears in the backcountry surrounding Lake Havasu City.

If you rent a boat, you can go up to Topock Gorge located eight miles north of Lake Havasu City. The gorge is situated within the Lake Havasu National Wildlife Refuge and offers fantastic scenery and ancient Indian petroglyphs.

If you're in town on Thanksgiving, watch the Havasu Classic Outboard World Championships. For information: 602-855-4115. The Desert Regatta is presented in May, and Boat and Ski Championships in June.

Attend the London Bridge Fiesta, a ten-day celebration held the first two weeks in October. Festivities include a parade, triathlon, costume contests and entertainment.

Pilots can fly into the airport by Havasu City and be right next to the Crazy Horse Campground which has showers and a camp store. Information: 602-855-4033 or 602-855-2127.

For information on desert walks, contact Desert Walks at 602-855-7055.
INFORMATION -
Lake Havasu State Park
1350 West McCulloch Blvd.
Lake Havasu City, Arizona 86403
602-855-7851

LOST DUTCHMAN STATE PARK
6

LOCATION - The park is northeast of Phoenix and six miles northeast of Apache Junction on Arizona 88. It's mostly visited during the cool winter months from November through April, with March being the most popular. Summertime months are usually too hot to enjoy the area.

ACTIVITIES - Stop by the visitor center and pick up a map of the hiking trails. The park has 35 undeveloped campsites and picnicking facilities. Picnic supplies are available both nearby and in Apache Junction.

A series of Forest Service hiking trails go from the park to the base of the Superstition Mountains. One of the trails, Siphon Draw, begins in the campground and follows the canyon to the face of the mountain. The trail ends after 1.6 miles, and you're faced with a more strenuous climb to the mountain top. If you do go hiking, watch out for the "jumping cholla." These really do "jump" if you get very close to the cactus, and you'll need pliers to remove them should they become embedded. The Superstition Mountains also offer additional hiking opportunities.

Guided hikes and campfire programs are available every Saturday from October through April. For information, call the park headquarters.

Horseback riders will find four stables in the Apache Junction area.

If you get the chance to read the story of the Lost Dutchman Mine, you'll find it adds a great deal to your explorations. Is there really a Lost Dutchman Mine just waiting to be found? Many have searched and met with mysterious deaths, but no one has been successful yet. The Dons Club in Phoenix conducts their annual "Lost Gold Trek" in March in an attempt to find the lost mine, but they haven't had much luck either.

INFORMATION -
Lost Dutchman State Park
6109 North Apache Trail
Apache Junction, Arizona 85219
602-982-4485

LYMAN LAKE STATE PARK
7

LOCATION - The park is 11 miles south of St. Johns and one mile east of U.S. 666. St. Johns has a municipal airport: 602-337-2000. The lake is located at 6,000 feet and is considered to be a perfect spring, summer and fall retreat.

ACTIVITIES - Enjoy year-round camping in one of 41 developed campsites, picnicking, hiking, swimming, boating and fishing for walleye, northern pike, channel catfish and crappie. Individual ramadas overlook the designated swimming area. Food service and boat rentals are available.

Duck and goose hunting is excellent here as the lake has the only open body of water in the latter part of the season. You can see a small buffalo herd at the park entrance.

You're 55 miles from the Petrified Forest National Park where you can see many huge petrified logs created when the logs were buried in sediments. Gradually, the wood was replaced with silica solutions, turning the wood into stone. The best area to tour is Long Logs because of its many good specimens.

INFORMATION -
Lyman Lake State Park
Box 1428
St. Johns, Arizona 85936
602-337-4441 or 337-4282

PAINTED ROCKS STATE PARK
8

LOCATION - Fifteen miles west of Gila Bend on I-8, and then 12 miles north on Painted Rocks Road.

ACTIVITIES - The park has two units. One features an outstanding collection of Indian rock drawings or petroglyphs located near the historic Gila Trail used by travelers going through Arizona since the 18th century. The other unit borders Painted Rocks Lake below Painted Rocks Dam where you can participate in water-based activities, hiking, fishing, swimming, picnicking or camping, but there is no drinking water in the campground. It's advisable to check on the water level in the lake because it's often dry.

INFORMATION -
Painted Rocks State Park
Star Route 1, Box 273
Gila Bend, Arizona 85337
602-683-2151

PATAGONIA LAKE
9

LOCATION - Twelve miles east of Nogales in the Sonoita Valley on Arizona 82 and then four miles north on a gravel road.

Since the park is at 3,750 feet, it has moderate temperatures throughout the year.

FEATURES - The lake was created by the damming of Sonoita Creek and is 2.5-miles long and 90 feet deep at the dam.

ACTIVITIES - Enjoy camping in one of the 95 developed sites, 10 with hookups, and 12 lake campsites which are only accessible by boat. Campers are encouraged to arrive early in the week since the campground fills up quickly on the weekends. Food service is available.

You can also have a picnic, go hiking along the .6-mile trail to Sonoita Creek, go boating, swimming and fishing for bass, crappie, bluegill and catfish during the summer. The lake is stocked with trout during the winter.

INFORMATION -
Patagonia Lake
Box 274
Patagonia, Arizona 85624
602-287-6965

PICACHO PEAK STATE PARK
10

LOCATION - Between Phoenix and Tucson, the park is 25 miles south of Casa Grande Ruins National Monument via Arizona 87 and 40 miles northwest of Tucson vai I-10.

ACTIVITIES - Picacho Peak rises sharply for 1,500 feet above the desert floor where a Civil War battle was fought. You can enjoy picnicking, camping or touring the visitor center in the desert mountain park. Because of the lush wildflower growth, spring is an excellent time to visit.

Hikers can tackle the route to the top of Picacho Peak, although inexperienced hikers are warned that the route is difficult. The trail begins at the parking area near Saguaro Ramada on Barrett Loop Drive and is two miles long with an elevation gain of 1,374 feet. A series of 15 iron posts and cables have been placed in spots where you'll cross bedrock or encounter steep pitches. This is a good place for you to reconsider whether or not the peak is worth the additional effort. Those deciding to go for the summit are advised to carry plenty of water, wear gloves to protect your hands while on the cables, and return the way you came.

In March, an annual reenactment of the Picacho Peak Civil War battle is presented by local historians.

You'll also be close to the Casa Grande Ruins National Monument which is in northern Coolidge off Arizona 87. This structure was built by the Hohokam Indians over 600 years ago and is open for touring. You can either take a self-guided tour or join one of the ranger talks.

INFORMATION -
Picacho Peak State Park
Box 275
Picacho, Arizona 85241
602-466-3183

ROPER LAKE STATE PARK
11

LOCATION -   Six miles south of Safford in southeastern Arizona, and then a half-mile east of U.S. 666.

ACTIVITIES - The park is located at the foot of Mount Graham, and its manmade lake is stocked with bass, bluegill and catfish. Picnic under a ramada by the shoreline which also has camp sites, a swimming beach, fishing dock and visitor center. Boaters are limited to sails, oars or electric motors.

Open for day use only, the Dankworth Unit is located six miles to the south.

INFORMATION -
Roper Lake State Park
Route 2, Box 712
Safford, Arizona 85546
602-428-6760

SLIDE ROCK STATE PARK
12

LOCATION - Seven miles north of Sedona on U.S. 89A.

ACTIVITIES - Enjoy hiking the trails in this picturesque area. They range in length from .7-mile to 5.6-miles up Wilson Mountain. The park is a favorite for swimmers.

Open for day use only, you can enjoy a picnic, go fishing in the stream or go camping in the nearby Forest Service campgrounds.

INFORMATION -
Slide Rock State Park
P.O. Box 10358
Sedona, Arizona 86336
602-282-3034

TOMBSTONE COURTHOUSE STATE HISTORICAL PARK
13

LOCATION - In Tombstone off U.S. 80 at 219 East Toughnut Street.

ACTIVITIES - The town of Tombstone was once called "The Town Too Tough to Die." It's most famous for the Earp-Clanton gunfight fought next to the OK Corral. A reenactment of the battle is presented on Sundays at 2:00 P.M. Information: 602-457-2227.

While the mining was good, it's said that the storekeepers had to sweep the bodies off their front steps when they opened for business. During its heyday, over $37,000,000 worth of silver was taken from the mines, and the town had a population of 15,000. By 1886, however, the mines had flooded and the boom was over.

Walk through Boot Hill graveyard to read the tombstones. They're fascinating.

The courthouse is at 219 E. Toughnut Street and was built in 1882. Walk through and see exhibits from the early days. Information: 602-457-3311.

Tour the Good Enough silver mine. For information: 602-457-3691.

Visit the old Bird Cage Theater, located at 6th and Allen, named for the 14 bird cage crib compartments used by the "ladies of the night" during its operation in 1889. The building was the site of 16 gunfights and has 140 bullet holes as evidence.

Pilots flying into town may be met by one of the town's citizens. When we landed in our Cessna 182, we were met by the sheriff who offered us a ride into town. Apparently they listen for the arrival of small planes and send someone out to the airport to bring their passengers into town. Maybe you'll be as lucky as we were.

INFORMATION -
Tombstone Courthouse State Historical Park
Box 216
Tombstone, Arizona 85638
602-457-3311

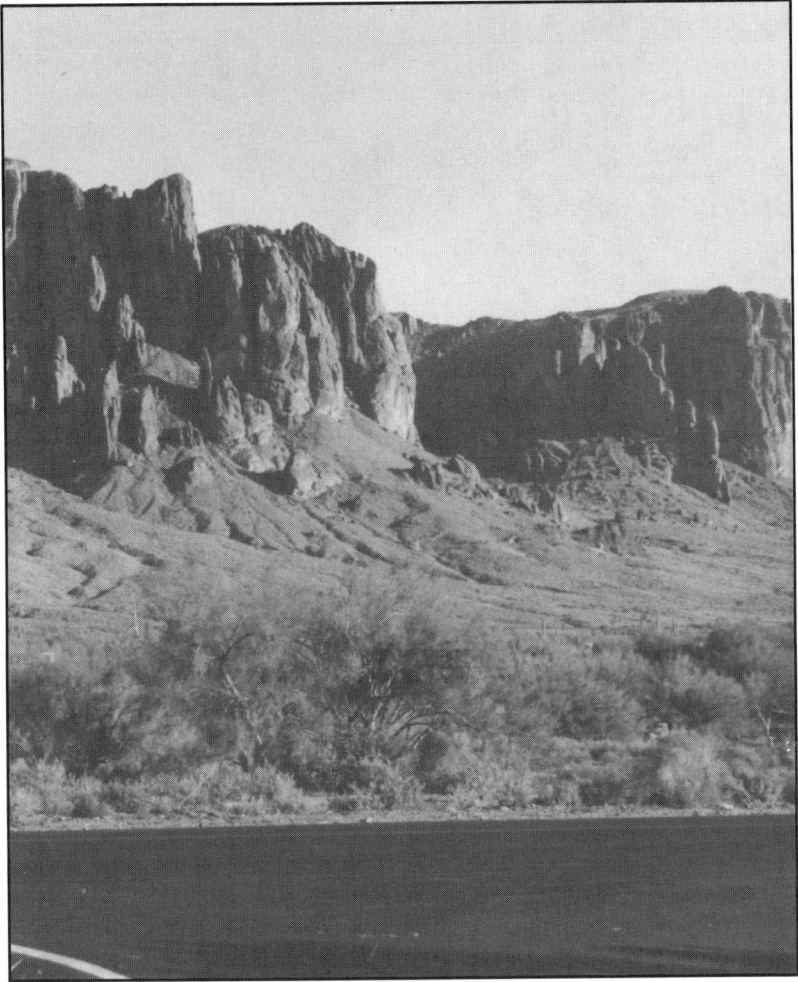

Superstition Mountains and Lost Dutchman State Park.
WARREN DEHAAN

"All aboard!" at Columbia State Park.

CALIFORNIA

Although California has 285 state park units, many are state beaches, and are not included here. The parks I've selected are divided into three areas: north of San Francisco, south of San Francisco, and the interior parks.

Camping is available in over 100 different parks and beaches, with summer being the busiest time. You can reserve campsites eight weeks in advance. For information on reservations: 1-800-952-5580. Mistix reservations: 1-800-446-7275 inside California, or 619-452-1950 outside California.

General park information may be obtained by calling 916-445-6477. State park information: 1-800-952-5580.

For additional information on the California State Parks or to obtain the map, "Guide to California State Parks", write to the Publications Division, California Department of Parks and Recreation, P.O. Box 2390, Sacramento, 95811. For a brochure, "State Parks of California — 1964 to the Present," write to the same address.

NORTH OF SAN FRANCISCO

REDWOOD STATE PARKS
1

The redwood parks stretch for 450 miles along the northern California coast from Oregon south to the Big Sur. Included along this stretch is the world's tallest redwood, reaching 367.8 feet. The parks offer the opportunity to walk

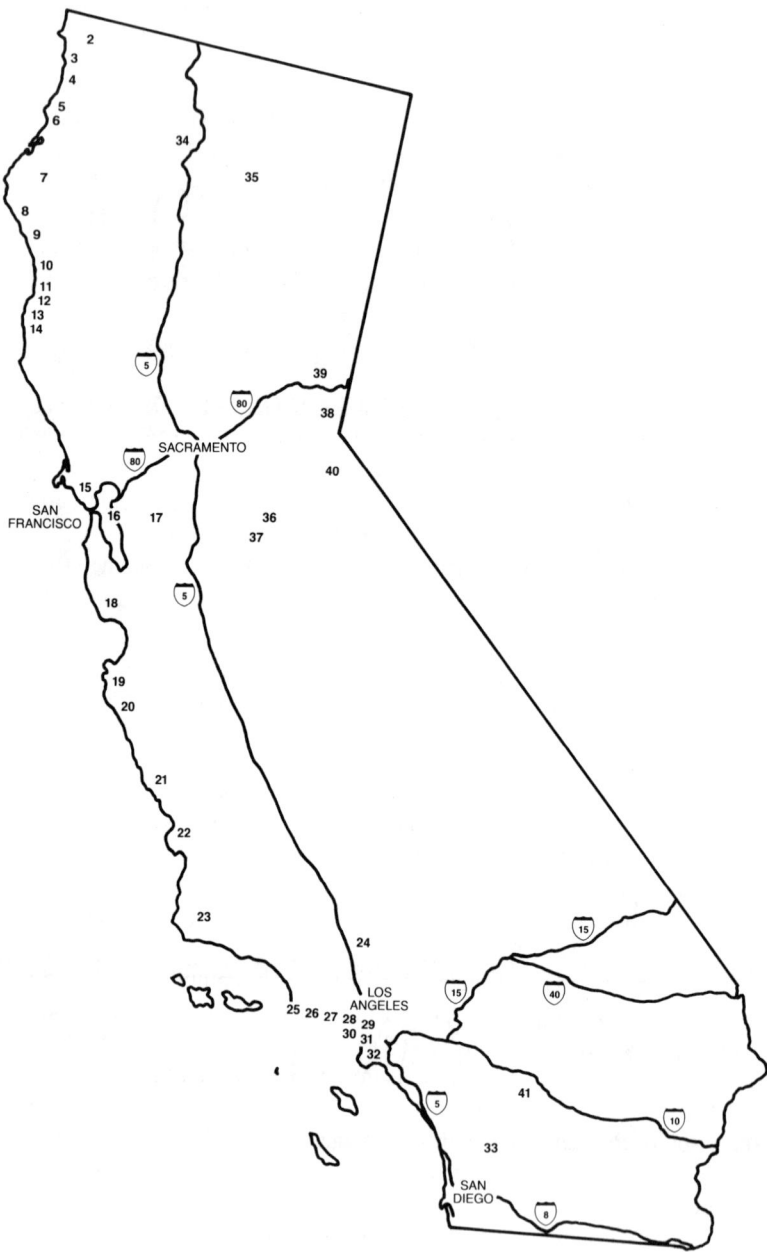

among 2,000-year-old, 300 feet tall trees. One of the most beautiful drives is along the Avenue of the Giants. The best stand of redwoods is found in Humboldt and Del Norte state parks.

The redwoods that grow along the coast are different from the redwoods found inland in the Sierras. The coastal trees are taller and thinner, averaging 350 feet in height, with a diameter of 20 feet. The giant sequoias, however, are shorter and thicker and can have a diameter of 35 feet. The sequoias live between 4,500 and 8,000 feet in elevation and can live to be as old as 3,500 years.

The area along the coast is noted for its rainfall. In fact, 174 feet was reported here one winter. Generally these rains begin in November and last through March.

Migrating whales head south past the parks in December and January, and then pass again as they return from Baja in March and April.

Fall and winter offer great salmon fishing, with the fish averaging 10-20 pounds each.

JEDEDIAH SMITH STATE PARK
2

LOCATION - Nine miles east of Crescent City on U.S. 199.

ACTIVITIES - The park has 15 memorial redwood groves which extend down steep slopes to the ocean. The world's largest measured redwood, reaching 16 feet in diameter and soaring 340 feet in the air, is found in Stout Grove. To see this tree, hike the Stout Grove Trail, a 30-minute walk. It's accessible from Howland Hill Road.

Two other scenic trails, Leiffer and Ellsworth, may be combined to give you a good sampling of the moss-laden trails of the area. The trailhead is on the left side of Walker Road, .4-mile from U.S. 199.

Another popular loop is the combination of Simpson and Peterson trails. Each is less than a mile in length, and together they provide you the opportunity to see many of the redwoods with their huge burls.

Visitors can also enjoy camping in one of 108 sites, picnicking, fishing and swimming.

Crescent City celebrates a Seafood Festival in September and the World Championship Crab races in February.

Redwoods National Park is located nearby where there are over 1,000 species of plants and animals along with the towering coastal redwoods. The world's tallest tree is found on the banks of Redwood Creek, and, when measured in 1964, was found to be 367.8 feet tall.

INFORMATION -
Jedediah Smith State Park
707-464-9533
    or
Klamath District
600-A Clark Street
Eureka, California 95501
707-445-6547

DEL NORTE COAST STATE PARK
3

LOCATION - The park is located eight miles south of Crescent City on U.S. 101.

FEATURES - This park has a thick growth of old redwoods, and its western side provides the visitor with access to the ocean beaches and tidepools. Flower lovers should come in the spring when the rhododendrons, some reaching as high as 30 feet, are blooming.

ACTIVITIES - Hike a 2.5-mile hiking trail, Damnation Creek Trail. It begins at Milepost 16 from U.S. 101 near False Klamath Cove and goes through the tall trees along shaded streams to a sheltered ocean cove.

Another longer trail, Last Chance Trail, goes for six miles, providing the hiker with some wonderful vistas of the seacoast. The trail begins at the end of Endert's Beach Road in the Crescent City section of the national park.

INFORMATION -
Del Norte Coast State Park
707-464-9533
    or
Klamath District
600-A Clark Street
Eureka, California 95501
707-445-6547

PRAIRIE CREEK REDWOOD STATE PARK
4

LOCATION - Six miles north of Orick on U.S. 101.

FEATURES - This is another coastal redwood state park, and has a resident herd of Roosevelt elk.

ACTIVITIES - Naturalists are on duty at the visitor center from Memorial Day through Labor Day. The park has 100 campsites spread between Elk Prairie Campground and Gold Bluffs Beach Campground. Reservations may be made by calling 800-446-PARK, or 619-452-1950.

While here you can go fishing, biking or hiking along over 70 miles of trails that crisscross the redwood forest, fern-covered ravines and beaches. The Gold Bluffs Beach hike is the easiest one — a 4.2-mile hike on the James Irvine Trail. Reaching the beach, considered one of the wildest along California's coast, involves driving a winding four-mile dirt road.

Another beautiful trail is along Fern Canyon, a .7-mile walk providing an opportunity to observe ferns clinging to 50-foot high canyon walls. This trail is only accessible during the summer, however, since the creek becomes impassable during the winter months.

INFORMATION -
Prairie Creek Redwood State Park
707-488-2171
    or
Region I Headquarters
3033 Cleveland Avenue, Suite 110
Santa Rosa, California 95403-2186
707-576-2185

HUMBOLDT LAGOONS STATE PARK
5

LOCATION - This park is four miles south of Orick on U.S. 101.

ACTIVITIES - The park surrounds two lagoons, Big Lagoon and Stone Lagoon. Both lagoons are separated from the ocean by narrow barrier beaches, but the ocean has succeeded in breaching the barriers, allowing fish to enter. As a result, there is good fishing year-round, especially for native cutthroat.

Enjoy the sandy beach, windsurfing, canoeing, collecting agates and driftwood, or exploring the lagoons. You can also tour the visitor center, picnic, camp in one of 25 campsites, or backpack into one of the hike-in campsites.

INFORMATION -
Humboldt Lagoons State Park
707-488-5435
    or
% Humboldt Redwoods State Park
P.O. Box 100

Weott, California 95571
707-946-2311

PATRICKS POINT STATE PARK
6

LOCATION - Five miles north of Trinidad on U.S 101.

FEATURES - The park is known for its agate beach and tidepools.

There is fog both night and morning year-round so the best season to visit is either spring or fall. The area receives 65 inches of annual rainfall, generally between October and April.

ACTIVITIES - Camping is available in 123 sites in Abalone, Penn Creek and Agate Beach Campgrounds. Reservations may be made by calling 1-800-I-Go-Park or 1-800-446-7275.

You can also enjoy a picnic, go hiking, rock climbing, fishing or tour the visitor center south of Agate Beach. Hike down the trail from here to fish for ling cod and trout.

Hike a three-kilometer Rim Trail which goes from the Agate Beach parking lot to Palmer's Point. There are other half-kilometer trails taking off from Rim Trail which lead down to the shoreline. Watch for gray whales passing by almost all year long.

South of Patricks Point is Abalone Point where the Yarok Indians inhabit a seasonal village.

INFORMATION -
Patricks Point State Park
707-677-3570
or
Region I Headquarters
3033 Cleveland Avenue, Suite 110
Santa Rosa, California 95403-2186
707-576-2185

GRIZZLY CREEK STATE PARK
7

LOCATION - This is a small park on California 36, seven miles east of Eureka on U.S. 101 and north of Humboldt Redwoods State Park.

FEATURES - The park was named for the now extinct grizzly that once inhabited the area.

ACTIVITIES - Grizzly Creek has 30 campsites and was once the noontime stop for stages traveling between Bridgeville and Strong's Station en route from San Francisco to Eureka.

The Van Duzen River runs through the park and offers salmon and steelhead fishing. Explore 4.5-miles of hiking trails, go camping, have a picnic, fish, swim and tour the visitor center. The rangers offer summer programs.

INFORMATION -
Grizzly Creek State Park
707-777-3683 or 946-2311
    or
% Humboldt Redwoods State Park
P.O. Box 100
Weott, California 95571
707-946-2311

HUMBOLDT REDWOODS STATE PARK
8

LOCATION - The park is one mile south of Weott and is on the Avenue of the Giants between Miranda and Redcrest on U.S. 101.

FEATURES - The most famous trees are the Dyerville Giant Tree, 362 feet; the Rockefeller Tree, 365 feet; and the Founders Tree, which reaches 346 feet. The average age of the trees is estimated to be between 800 and 1500 years.

The area is often foggy during the summer and winter, making spring and fall better times to visit.

ACTIVITIES - Visitors can tour the visitor center, ride horseback, picnic, swim, fish, camp in one of 247 sites, or in one of six backpacking sites including Johnson Camp which has four rustic cabins available for overnight rentals. Camping is also available in Scotia, Redcrest, Myers Flat, Phillipsville, Redway and Garberville.

Enjoy 100 miles of hiking trails which wind through the redwood groves and open meadows, and tour the largest redwood mill in the world.

Fishermen can enjoy trout fishing from May through November in the Eel and Mattoll rivers. Salmon run in the King and Silvers rivers from November through January, and steelhead run from December through April.

Rockhounds can find jade and jasper along the south fork of the Eel River, plus additional jade along the beaches.

A nearby attraction is the Avenue of the Giants, a 33-mile section of highway which parallels U.S. 101 between Phillipsville and Pepperwood along the Eel River. This section of redwoods is the site of an annual marathon.

INFORMATION -
Humboldt Redwoods State Park
P.O. Box 100
Weott, California 95571
707-946-2311, or 946-2273 (summers only)

RICHARDSON GROVE STATE PARK
9

LOCATION - Eight miles south of Garberville on U.S. 101.

ACTIVITIES - Camp in one of 170 sites with no hookups. Camping supplies are available in the camp store.

Huckleberry Campground is on the west side of U.S. 101 and is set aside for bikers and hikers. Boat rentals are available in nearby Benbow Lake State Recreation Area, three miles south of Garberville.

Enjoy fishing for chinook, silver salmon, steelhead trout, sucker fish and lampreys. The rainy season offers the best fishing since spawning activities occur from October through February. Summer fishing isn't as good because of low water and smaller fish. The king salmon runs start in October and continue into December. You'll need a fishing license. For current fishing information, contact the North Coast Fishphone: 707-442-8552.

You can also enjoy some good hiking among the trees or go swimming in the surf.

INFORMATION -
Richardson Grove State Park
707-247-3318 or 946-2311
or
Region I Headquarters
3033 Cleveland Avenue, Suite 110
Santa Rosa, California 95403-2186
707-576-2185

SINKYONE WILDERNESS STATE PARK
10

LOCATION - 30 miles west of Redway on County Road 435, Briceland Road, or 50 miles north of Fort Bragg via California 1 and County Road 431. The latter access is a dirt road and is not maintained.

It's also 20 miles west of Garberville. The last nine miles, however, are unpaved and sometimes steep.

The state park is near Shelter Cove which has a small airstrip and camping on the field.

ACTIVITIES - Since this is a wilderness park, it is wild, rustic and generally undeveloped. It has 22 primitive, backpacking campsites only. Carry your own water. Obtain a camping permit at the visitor center.

At the south end of the park is Usal Beach, 10 miles north of Rockport via six miles of rugged and unpaved road.

INFORMATION -
Sinkyone Wilderness State Park
Eel River District Headquarters
P.O. Box 100
Weott, California 95571
707-946-2311

MACKERRICHER STATE PARK
11

LOCATION - Three miles north of Fort Bragg on California 1.

ACTIVITIES - While in Fort Bragg, plan to ride "The Skunks" train to see the redwoods. The depot is off Main Street and Laurel Avenue. For information and reservations: 707-964-6371, or write California West Railroad, P.O. Box 907, Fort Bragg, California, 95437. The railroad operates two passenger trains with open observation cars called "Super Skunks." During the summer these trains make two round trips daily to Northspur. Snacks are available at Northspur and the round trip takes three hours. Trains leave Fort Bragg at 9:20 A.M. and at 1:00, 3:00, and 5:00 P.M.

You can take a longer train trip by starting from Willits, 40 miles away. This trip takes 7.5-hours and crosses 31 bridges and trestles as it goes into the redwood forest.

Bicycle rentals are available from Fort Bragg Cyclery on South Franklin: 707-964-3509.

INFORMATION -
Mackerricher State Park
707-937-5804
   or
Mendocino District
P.O. Box 440
Mendocino, California 95460
707-937-5804

RUSSIAN GULCH STATE PARK
12

LOCATION - Two miles north of Mendocino on California 1.
ACTIVITIES - Camping or bicycling along a three-mile bicycle trail.
INFORMATION -
Russian Gulch State Park
P.O. Box 440
Mendocino, California 95460
707-937-5804

MENDOCINO HEADLANDS STATE PARK
13

LOCATION - The park surrounds the town of Mendocino in northern California.

ACTIVITIES - Walk the spectacular nature trail along the headlands next to the town. Look down steep cliffs to watch the ocean crashing below you. The wildflowers along the trail are magnificent.

Hike down to the beach for some swimming. Bicycling along here is also quite beautiful. Rental bicycles are available from Mendocino Cyclery on Main Street: 707-937-4744.

Pilots who fly into the Little River Airport in the spring during rhododendron blossoming time can hike down to the river from the edge of the runway where they can arrange to be picked up and returned to their plane. Arrangements may be made with the Mendocino Stage Shuttle: 707-964-0167. The hike takes the better part of the day, depending upon how often you stop to enjoy the beautiful surroundings. Car rentals are available at the strip: 707-937-1224. Reservations are suggested.

Rent cabins in the nearby outdoor center nestled in the redwoods seven miles from town. Reservations and information: Mendocino Woodlands Camp Association, P.O. Box 267, Mendocino, California 95460, or call 707-937-5755.

Camping is available in four campgrounds.
INFORMATION -
Mendocino Headlands State Park
P.O. Box 440
Mendocino, California 95460
707-937-5804

VAN DAMME STATE PARK
14

LOCATION - Three miles south of Mendocino on California 1.

ACTIVITIES - Go hiking, camping in one of 74 sites, or bicycling along the three-mile bicycle trail.

INFORMATION -
Van Damme State Park
P.O. Box 440
Mendocino, California 95460
707-937-5804

MOUNT TAMALPAIS STATE PARK
15

LOCATION - Six miles west of Mill Valley on Panoramic Highway, and north of San Francisco and the Golden Gate Bridge.

FEATURES - Mount Tamalpais rises 2,571 feet and combines urban and natural scenery. The park surrounds the Muir Woods National Monument and is bordered by the Golden Gate National Recreational Area on the south. The profile you can see on the mountain summit is believed to resemble a sleeping Indian maiden.

In 1884, the Mill Valley and Tamalpais Scenic Railroad laid a track to the top of the mountain, billed as the "crookedest railroad in the world," with 281 curves in over eight-miles plus boasting a five-fold switchback. Following a fire on the mountain, the railroad stopped its operations in the 1930s.

ACTIVITIES - Drive or hike to the top of the mountain. The hike is 8.5-miles and begins at the Pantoll Ranger Station. From here, you can watch hanggliders taking off from the summit to soar down to the valley.

The park has a total of 40 miles of hiking trails including a two-mile hike to the Mountain Theater where a variety of special events are presented. Besides hiking, you can go camping, picnicking, fishing, horseback riding or backpacking. Lee Stransky Backpack Camp is two miles south of the Pantoll Ranger Station and has 16 sites but no water. Reservations: 415-388-2070. Camping is also available in Steep Ravine, one mile south of Stinson Beach. It has 10 rustic cabins which may be reserved. For information, call 415-456-5218 or 388-2070. Food is available in the park.

INFORMATION -
Mount Tamalpais State Park
P.O. Box 34159

San Francisco, California 94134
415-388-2070 or 557-4069

ANGEL ISLAND STATE PARK
16

LOCATION - Take a ferry from either Tiburon or San Francisco.

FEATURES - At one time, the area was used as an immigrant quarantine station, Nike missile base, and a military overseas staging area.

ACTIVITIES - Go camping, picnicking, fishing, hiking, boating and hiking on the nature trail. Food service is available. During the summer, you can take a train tour.

INFORMATION -
Angel Island State Park
415-456-5218
   or
P.O. Box 34159
San Francisco, California 94134
415-557-4069

MOUNT DIABLO STATE PARK
17

LOCATION - The park is northeast of San Francisco. Go east for five miles from Danville on I-680 east.

ACTIVITIES - Tour the visitor center, picnic, horseback ride, drive or hike to the mountain summit of 3,849 feet. On a clear day, the view from the top enables you to see 35 of California's 58 counties, Lassen Peak and the Golden Gate Bridge. Besides this hike, the area has over 100 miles of other hiking and horseback riding trails. Rangers offer guided hikes as well, so check the schedule at the park headquarters to see what's available.

If you decide to camp in one of 60 sites, you can make reservations through Mistix up to eight weeks in advance for visits from October 1-May 31. During the summer, however, the sites are available on a first-come, first-served basis.

The best time to visit is during the spring when the wildflowers are quite spectacular. Summers are hot and dry, and sometimes the peak even gets snow during the winter.

INFORMATION -
Mount Diablo State Park

415-837-2525
or
P.O.Box 34159
San Francisco, California 94134
415-557-4069

SOUTH OF SAN FRANCISCO

BIG BASIN REDWOODS STATE PARK
18

LOCATION - Twenty miles northeast of Santa Cruz via California 9 and 236.

FEATURES - The climate here is moderate with early morning summer fog and occasional winter snows. The redwood trees measure 18 feet in diameter and reach 330 feet.

ACTIVITIES - Visit the natural museum and visitor center. You can also enjoy a picnic, or do some great hiking along 100 miles of trails. Some of the trails go within the groves of giant trees, while others follow the rugged ocean shoreline. Be sure to hike the Redwood Nature Trail to see a stand of virgin redwoods rising over 300 feet.

The park has 188 campsites, which may be reserved year-round through Ticketron. It also has six backpacking sites for which reservations are required. For these sites, contact the park headquarters. You can also enjoy a horseback ride and camping overnight in the horse trail campground. Reservations: 408-425-1218.

INFORMATION -
Big Basin Redwoods State Park
21600 Big Basin Way
Boulder Creek, California, 95006
408-338-6132

POINT LOBOS STATE RESERVE
19

LOCATION - Three miles south of Carmel Bay on California 1.

ACTIVITIES - The area is described as the "greatest meeting between land and water in the world." Watch for California sea otters floating past on their backs in the kelp beds. In November, gray whales pass by here on their way to breeding and calving grounds in lower California as part of their 2,000-mile journey.

Look for the Sea Lion rock formation offshore where you can see California and Stellar's sea lions. You can also spot Bird Island and the Pinnacles from here. Watch for the picturesque twisted Grove Monterrey cypress trees growing in the area.

Many hiking trails lace the preserve. One hike goes along the shoreline at Sea Lion Point and between Sand Hill Cove and Pebbly Beach. Scuba divers go to Whaler's and Bluefish coves.

INFORMATION -
Point Lobos State Reserve
Route 1, Box 62
Carmel, California 93923
408-624-4909

PFEIFFER-BIG SUR STATE PARK
20

LOCATION - The park is on the Big Sur River, 26 miles south of Carmel on California 1.

ACTIVITIES - The park has a visitor center, lodge and food service available.

One of the hiking trails, 4.5-miles long, climbs 3,000 feet up Mount Manuel. Other trails lead to waterfalls, groves, gorges, sea caverns and lagoons. Enjoy swimming, fishing and camping in one of 217 campsites or attend one of the campfire programs provided by naturalists during the summer.

INFORMATION -
Pfeiffer-Big Sur State Park, No. 1
Big Sur, California 93920
408-667-2317

HEARST SAN SIMEON STATE HISTORIC MONUMENT
21

LOCATION - On California 1 in San Simeon, 42 miles north of San Luis Obispo.

FEATURES - The monument contains the castle, guesthouses and grounds once occupied by the late William Randolph Hearst. The castle has millions of dollars' worth of Hearst's art collection and antiques. The grounds surrounding the castle are beautiful.

ACTIVITIES - Tours are given daily from 8-3 except Thanksgiving, Christmas or New Year's Day. For tour reservations, contact Mistix: 805-952-5580 (in California) or 619-452-1950 (out of state.) The tour cost $8.00 in 1988. If you plan to charge your ticket by phone, call 800-446-7275 (in California) or 619-452-1950 (out of state). The tours last approximately an hour and forty-five minutes. Four different tours are offered, but tour number one gives the best overview of the castle.

You can't park at the museum unless you've made prior reservations. Park at the visitor center off California 1 and take the tour bus five miles up to the museum. While waiting for the bus, walk through the center to see exhibits on Hearst and the estate's principal architect, Julia Morgan.

INFORMATION -
Hearst San Simeon State Historic Monument
P.O. Box 8
San Simeon, California 93452-0040
805-927-2020 or 927-4621

MORRO BAY STATE PARK
22

LOCATION - The park is located in southern California south of Morro Bay on California 1.

ACTIVITIES - Morro Bay State Park is a well-known marine area and has a beautiful lagoon and bay to explore. Tour the museum of natural history, enjoy camping in one of 30 sites, picnicking, fishing, hiking, swimming, sailing, taking nature walks or attending interpretive programs.

Ride aboard the sternwheeler, Tigers Folly. For information, call 805-772-2257 or 772-2255.

INFORMATION -
Morro Bay State Park
805-772-2560

or
Region 4 Headquarters
1333 Camino Del Rio South, Suite 200
San Diego, California 92108
619-237-7411

LA PURISIMA MISSION STATE HISTORIC PARK
23

LOCATION - The park is four miles northeast of Lompoc on Purisima Road and north of Santa Barbara.

FEATURES - The mission was first begun in 1787 at a site three miles south of here, but severe earthquakes destroyed the original building in 1812. The mission is connected to the other California missions by the El Camino Real, the "Royal Highway." It's the 11th in a string of missions that extended from San Diego to Sonoma and was originally established to control the coastal Indians.

ACTIVITIES - Tour the grounds, hike along 13 miles of nature trails, or go horseback riding. Guided tours of the mission are given by appointment. Nine buildings have been restored, and the rooms are furnished as they were in the 1820s. During the summer you can watch demonstrations of early mission crafts.

The museum has a good Indian artifact collection and exhibits from the mission. It's open Tuesday-Friday 1-5, and Saturday-Sunday 1-4. For information, call 805-736-3888.

A major fiesta is held the third Sunday in May. Information: 805-733-3713

INFORMATION -
La Purisima Mission State Historic Park
RFD Box 102
Lompoc, California 93436
805-733-3713

FORT TEJON STATE HISTORIC PARK
24

LOCATION - The park is in Grapevine Canyon on the I-5 "Ridge Route," 77 miles north of Los Angeles and 36 miles south of Bakersfield.

To reach the park from the south, take the Fort Tejon Historic Park exit from I-5, four miles north of Lebec. Follow the exit road a quarter of a mile to the parking lot.

From the north, leave the freeway five miles south of Grapevine at the Fort Tejon exit. It's one more block to the park.

FEATURES - This fort is unique because it was built without any fortification walls. Its primary mission was to protect the Indians rather than fight them. Ironically, it became the headquarters for the Army's most elite Indian fighters, the dragoons. These heavily armed horsemen had two special privileges: the right to wear rakish French-styled uniforms and the right to grow mustaches.

It was also the training center for the U.S. Army's first and only Camel Corps. These camels ridden by the dragoons rode camel-escort for the miners, chased bandits, and even established a camel mail run to Los Angeles, involving a round trip of 150 miles.

ACTIVITIES - If you arrive here on the third Sunday of each month from April through October, you can watch the 500 member Fort Tejon Historical Association riding horseback and staging three pitched battles at the old fort. These occur at 11:00 A.M., 1:00 and 3:00 P.M.

On the first Sunday of the month year-round, this group creates a "Living History of Fort Tejon" with an encampment in period costumes on the fort's parade grounds.

Take a self-guided tour of the small museum, the barracks and officers' quarters.

INFORMATION -
Fort Tejon State Historic Park
P.O. Box 895
Lebec, California 93243
805-248-6447

POINT MUGU STATE PARK
25

LOCATION - Fifteen miles south of Oxnard on California 1, and 32 miles northeast of Santa Monica.

ACTIVITIES - Go camping in one of 56 developed sites at the Big Sycamore Campground or in one of 102 primitive sites at La Jolla Beach Campground. La Jolla Valley also has 12 hiker/biker campsites. Reservations are necessary for Big Sycamore and La Jolla Beach Campgrounds between March 1 and November 30. Call Mistix: 1-800-I-Go-Park.

Bicycles may ride the fire roads, sharing them with hikers. Horseback riders can enter the park via Newbury Park. You can also picnic, fish or go swimming in the ocean. The beach closes at dusk.

INFORMATION -
Point Mugu State Park
9000 Pacific Coast Highway
Oxnard, California
818-987-3303, 706-1310, or 805-488-5223

LEO CARILLO STATE BEACH
26

LOCATION - Twenty-one miles southeast of Oxnard and 25 miles northeast of Santa Monica where the Mulholland Highway intersects the Pacific Coast Highway, California 1.

ACTIVITIES - Hike along 11 miles of hiking trails, enjoy a picnic on the beach where stoves are provided, go swimming, surfing, and tidepooling in the ocean where lifeguards are on duty at certain times. Attend campfire programs, go on nature walks, and tour the interpretive trailer. There is a camp store and a sanitation dump station.

Camping is available in 16 hiker/biker sites and in one of 138 tent sites. Thirty-two developed beach sites are available for tents and self-contained vehicles.

INFORMATION -
Leo Carillo State Beach
35000 Pacific Coast Highway
Malibu, California 90265
805-488-5223

MALIBU CREEK STATE PARK
27

LOCATION - Four miles south of U.S. 101 on Las Virgenes/Malibu Canyon Road, Calabasas. The main entrance is 200 yards south of the Mulholland Highway. Take the Las Virgenes exit from the south Ventura Freeway, California 1. From the Pacific Coast Highway, California 1, go north on Malibu Canyon Road for approximately six miles.

FEATURES - The area was once owned by Ronald Reagan and Bob Hope, and more recently has been used for the filming of over 200 movies.

CLIMATE - Wintertime temperatures range from lows in the 20s and highs in the 70s. Summertime highs can reach 100 degrees, but drop into the low 70s at night. Most of the area's rainfall arrives from mid-November through mid-April.

ACTIVITIES - Go fishing for catfish, bass, bluegill or for trout stocked in the creek. Fishing is only good from January through May. After this, the water levels are too low. Hike on 30 miles of hiking trails or ride mountain bicycles or horses on the fire roads. The campground has 66 campsites with water and showers, but no hookups. Trailers are limited to 18 feet or less.

Take a picnic to enjoy in the Reagan picnic area or visit the former M*A*S*H set on Crags Road.

During the summer the park is subject to periodic closures due to high fire danger. To avoid visiting the park then, call 818-706-1310.

INFORMATION -
Malibu Creek State Park
28754 Mulholland Highway
Agoura, California 91301
818-706-1310 or 213-706-8809

MALIBU LAGOON STATE BEACH
28

LOCATION - The beach is next to the Pacific Coast Highway, California 1, at Cross Creek Road.

ACTIVITIES - The area is regularly visited by various classes of elementary school age students through college level because of its diverse fish and bird life. Interpretive panels give information about the lagoon.

The parking lot provides access to Malibu's famous Surfrider beach. Picnicking facilities are available.

INFORMATION -
Malibu Lagoon State Beach
23200 Pacific Coast Highway
Malibu, California 90265
213-456-9497

LOS ENCINOS STATE HISTORIC PARK
29

LOCATION - From the Ventura Freeway, U.S. 101, exit at Balboa and proceed south onto Balboa Boulevard toward Ventura Boulevard. Moorpark Street is on the left.

ACTIVITIES - Visit the spring-fed reservoir which is a haven for ducks and fish. You can purchase duck food in the park. Purchase a map to take a self-guided tour of the property which includes the original buildings from the Rancho El Encino. Bring along a picnic.

INFORMATION -
Los Encinos State Historic Park
16756 Moorpark Street
Encino, California 91436
818-784-4849

TOPANGA STATE PARK
30

LOCATION - The park lies within the city limits of Los Angeles. It's the nation's second largest urban park and the world's largest wildland situated within the boundaries of a major city. To reach the park, follow Topanga Canyon Boulevard, California 27, south from the Ventura Freeway, U.S. 101, or go north from the Pacific Coast Highway, California 1, to Entrada Road. There may not be any park signs at this point, so look for the Entrada Road entrance across from the Sassafrass Nursery. Follow Entrada for approximately one more mile to reach the main park entrance at the Trippet Ranch day-use area.

ACTIVITIES - The area has 32-miles of hiking trails. One of them goes from the park to Will Rogers State Park, 9.4-miles away. You can also hike the nature trail using the self-guiding booklet available at the trailhead. Go bicycling and horseback riding on the fire roads.

A hike-in campsite with eight units is located one mile from the Trippet Ranch on the Musch Trail. Register at the Trippet Ranch Ranger Station.

Nature walks and interpretive programs are offered at the ranch. Call the park or check the bulletin board for the schedule. Picnicking facilities are also available.

INFORMATION -
Topanga State Park
20825 Entrada Road
Topanga, California 90290
213-455-2465

WILL ROGERS STATE HISTORIC PARK
31

LOCATION - The park is on the edge of the Santa Monica Mountains in Pacific Palisades. From the San Diego freeway, U.S. 405, go west on Sunset Boulevard for approximately five miles to intersect Will Rogers Road. If approaching from the Pacific Coast Highway, California 1, follow Sunset Boulevard through downtown Pacific Palisades and turn left on Will Rogers Road. The park's address is 14253 Sunset Boulevard.

FEATURES - During the 1920s, Will Rogers built his ranch here above Sunset Boulevard. Originally only a small weekend cottage, it was gradually expanded to its current size of 31 rooms.

ACTIVITIES - The park grounds are open from 8:00 A.M. until 7:00 P.M. during the summer, and until 6:00 P.M. during the winter. Will Rogers' home is open daily from 10:00 A.M. until 5:00 P.M. except on holidays.

Tour his historic ranch to see memorabilia from his life or have a picnic on the grounds. Rangers give talks in the house and lead nature hikes and grounds tours on the weekend.

You can also watch a film on his life, hike a three-kilometer loop to Inspiration Point, or continue for 9.5-miles to reach Topanga Canyon. This trail leaves from Inspiration Point.

Bicyclists can ride along the paved roads or on the fire road. A game of polo is played year-round on Saturday from 2-5, and on Sunday from 10-1.

INFORMATION -
Will Rogers State Historic Park
15253 Sunset Boulevard
Pacific Palisades, California 90272
213-454-8212

J. PAUL GETTY MUSEUM
32

LOCATION - 17985 Pacific Coast Highway in Malibu between Sunset and Topanga Canyon Boulevard. It's approximately 25 miles west of Los Angeles.

FEATURES - Although the museum isn't a state park, it is a "must" for anyone who enjoys art and beautiful grounds. Temperatures along the coast are generally 10 degrees cooler than inland.

ACTIVITIES - Museum hours are from 10-5 Tuesday through Sunday. It's closed Monday and major holidays.

Admission is free, but you are prohibited from parking along the residential streets by the museum. If you want to use the parking garage located on the premises, make your reservation at least two weeks in advance: 213-458-2003. Otherwise, you can park by the Chart House Restaurant on the coast and catch the shuttle to the museum. It runs approximately every 15 minutes.

The museum is a true show place and is a re-creation of an ancient Roman country house. It has colorful gardens and a fascinating art collection. Short orientation talks are given every 15 minutes from 9:45-3:00 near the visitor center. You can also attend longer talks on the various exhibits. Check the schedule near the information desk adjacent to the book store.

Public lectures are presented Thursday evenings. For information and reservations: 213-458-2003.

INFORMATION -
J. Paul Getty Museum
17985 Pacific Coast Highway
Malibu, California 90406
213-458-2003

PALOMAR MOUNTAIN STATE PARK
33

LOCATION - Drive north from Escondido on California 86, then five miles east on California 76. To reach the park, continue north nine miles on California 86, and then west for three more miles on California 87.

FEATURES - The park houses the large Hale telescope along with three other smaller telescopes.

ACTIVITIES - Besides being able to see the 200 inch Hale telescope from the visitors' gallery every day from 9-4, you can also see many good photos of the celestial bodies in the Greenway Museum. While here, you can go camping, picnicking, and hiking.

INFORMATION -
Palomar Mountain State Park
714-742-3462
% Ocotillo Wells District
P.O. Box 360
Borrego Springs, California 92004
619-767-5391

INTERIOR PARKS

CASTLE CRAGS STATE PARK
34

LOCATION - Six miles south of Dunsmuir off U.S. I-5.

FEATURES - Granite crags tower over the Sacramento River where you can enjoy camping in one of 64 sites, picnicking, fishing, hiking, swimming and attending naturalist programs on Wednesday and Saturday from Memorial Day through Labor Day.

INFORMATION -
Castle Crags State Park
916-235-2684 or 225-2065
   or
Region 3 Headquarters
P.O. Box 1450
Lodi, California 95241-1450
209-333-6901

MCARTHUR-BURNEY FALLS MEMORIAL STATE PARK
35

LOCATION - This park is near Pit River in northeast California, half way between Mount Shasta and Lassen Peak. It's 11 miles north of Burney on California 89.

FEATURES - Burney Falls was called the Eighth Wonder of the World by President Theodore Roosevelt. The waterfalls are part of the original Pit River Falls which have been eroding away the underlying rock as they move upstream.

North and south of the park you can see some small, steep-sided volcanoes or cinder cones. Because of the volcanic activity in the area, visitors can also see small subterranean holes, tubes and caverns such as Subway Cave located along California 89, south of the park. The cavern was formed when lava continued to flow on the inside of the tube after the outside had hardened.

The park is especially popular from early June through late September when the days are warm and sunny and the nights cool.

ACTIVITIES - Hike one mile to the falls which drop 129 feet into Burney Creek. Fish for trout in Hat Creek and in nearby Fall River, Baum, Eastman and Big Lakes. Crappie, catfish and bass are stocked in Lake Britton.

Camp, picnic, hike, go boating where boat rentals are available, or swim in Lake Britton from a large sandy beach. Food service is provided.

A nearby attraction is Lassen Volcanic National Park, only 40 minutes away from here. Visitors can see many amazing volcanic features including hot springs, mud pots, thermal springs, and the remains of the ancient volcano, Mount Tehama. This park is a hikers' haven with over 100 miles of trails awaiting your exploration.

INFORMATION -

McArthur-Burney Falls Memorial State Park
Route 1, Box 1260
Burney, California, 96013
916-335-2777

CALAVARAS BIG TREES STATE PARK
36

LOCATION - Four miles east of Arnold on California 4.

ACTIVITIES - Tour the visitor center, attend interpretative summer programs, and go fishing or swimming.

The grove contains approximately 150 giant Sierra sequoias. Hike the 600-foot long "Three Senses Trail" which wanders through the North Grove. Another trail, South Grove, is located one mile from the end of the paved road at Beaver Creek. This trail continues two more miles to the headwaters of Big Trees Creek. It descends 1,500 feet to the river where there is a parking area if you want to arrange to be picked up there rather than hike back up the hill.

Another trail begins at the Lava Bluffs Parking Area and goes along the south facing slope above the Stanislaus River. Besides these trails, the park offers several fire roads to explore.

There are picnic facilities at North Grove and Beaver Creek, with less formal ones located along the Stanislaus River. One-hundred-twenty-nine campsites are located in the park, with one in North Grove, another in Oak Hollow plus some primitive backpacking campsites. Contact the park authorities for information and reservations. You can make reservations up to eight weeks in advance by calling MISTIX: 800-446-PARK, or inside California:

619-452-1950. In person reservations may be made Monday through Saturday at any MISTIX outlet. To find the one closest to you: 800-952-5580.

INFORMATION -
Calavaras Big Trees State Park
P.O. Box 120
Arnold, California, 95223
209-795-2334

COLUMBIA STATE HISTORIC PARK
37

LOCATION - The park is in Columbia, southwest of Calavaras State Park and near Yosemite National Park. It's located in the old business district in town.

FEATURES - Gold was discovered here in 1850. Columbia was referred to as "The Gem of the Southern Mines" since over $1.5 billion worth of gold (in today's currency) was mined here. At its peak, there were over 5,000 inhabitants, 150 saloons, shops and other businesses. The town was destroyed by fire twice. Its second rebuilding was done using fireproof brick.

The area covers 12 blocks and includes buildings which have been partially restored to their original gold rush appearance.

ACTIVITIES - The old City Hotel still offers accommodations. For reservations: 209-532-1478. Tour the museum to learn more of the history.

Attend a play in the Fallon Theater Tuesday through Saturdays at 8:30, or Saturday and Sunday at 2:00 P.M., mid-June through mid-August. For summer reservations, call 209-532-4644. The rest of the year, call 209-946-2116.

Take a free stagecoach ride in the 100-year-old stagecoach. For information: 209-532-4301.

Many special activities are conducted throughout the year including an Easter parade, a rose show on Mother's Day, Columbia Diggin's Living History held the first Sunday in June; Columbia Fly-in held the third weekend in June; Antique show on the fourth Sunday in June; Fiddle and Banjo contest held the second Saturday in October, and the Docent Lamplight Tour scheduled for the first Saturday in December.

A nearby attraction is nine miles north of Columbia on Perrotts Ferry Road. Three tours, each 45 minutes long, are offered daily through Moaning Caverns. You can do "The Rappell," a rope descent, or take a three-hour adventure tour by reservation: 209-736-2708.

The airport located one mile southwest of town has a campground for pilots. Information: 209-533-5685. Camping is also available in the 49er Trailer Ranch and RV Park: 209-532-9898.

INFORMATION -
Columbia State Historic Park
P.O. Box 151
Columbia, California 95310
209-532-4301

LAKE TAHOE
38

Lake Tahoe is the largest alpine lake in North America. It has a 72-mile shoreline and is over 1,600 feet deep in some places. The airport is located near South Tahoe and has rental cars available on the field.

During the summer the temperatures are in the 70s during the daytime and 40s at night. During the winter, the high is in the 40s with lows in the 20s. The state parks are closed during the winter, but open in late May and remain open through mid-September.

ACTIVITIES - Three paddlewheelers ply the waters of Lake Tahoe. The Tahoe Queen has a glass bottom and departs daily at 11:00 A.M., 1:30 and 3:55 P.M. from June through October, and at noon the rest of the year. Sunset dinner cruises are available as well. Reservations: 916-541-3364

The M.S. Dixie cruises from Zephyr Cove, Nevada, to Emerald Bay at 11:00 A.M. and 2:00 P.M. from mid-June through mid-September, and at noon the rest of the year. Reservations: 702-588-3509 (South Shore) 702-882-0786 (North Shore)

North Tahoe Cruises leave from the Round House Mall and Marina in Tahoe City off California 28 at 700 North Lake Boulevard. It takes you on a two hour historic trip along the northwest shore of the lake at 11:00 A.M., 1:30 and 3:30 P.M. from mid-May through Mid-October. Sunset cruises leave Monday through Saturday at 6:00. Reservations: 916-583-0141

On Memorial Day, attend the annual race between the Tahoe Queen and the M.S. Dixie.

Watch rainbow trout and kokanee salmon in an underground viewing chamber. The Stream Profile Chamber is located two-thirds of a mile down Rainbow Trail at the Forest Service Visitor Center and is open daily during the summer and fall.

On the southwest shore, tour Tallac Historic Site located between Fallen Leaf Road and Camp Richardson, and return in the evening for a living history program. Music lovers can attend evening jazz concerts, chamber music concerts on Sunday evenings, or if you're in town in July-August, listen to the special bluegrass concerts presented at the Valhalla Estate.

For information on the Lake Tahoe Summer Music Festival at Tahoe City, call 916-583-7625. For information on the North Lake Tahoe music series held at Incline Village, call 702-831-4622.

For water activities, you can jet ski, canoe, sail, kayak, water ski and swim from 20 beaches with 12 specifically designated for swimming. Even the water close to shore is very cold, however, with an average surface temperature of around 60 degrees during the summer.

You can parasail at Kings Beach, or ride the cable car at Squaw Valley from mid-June through October from 10-4.

Rental bicycles are available in Tahoe City at 1785 West Lake Boulevard, and at Sunnyside. A bicycle campground is located in Blackwood Canyon north of Homewood, with another one at Kaspian, five miles south of Tahoe City.

A bike trail begins at General Creek south of Sugar Pine Point State Park, and continues past Tahoe City. If you're feeling ambitious, cycle up to Donner Lake State Park. When we drove around the lake, we saw bicyclists everywhere, but the east side has no riding shoulder, making cycling hazardous.

You'll find more accommodations on the west side of the lake than on the east side where they become more widely separated. Campgrounds are scattered all around the lake, but again are more numerous on the west side.

Fifteen trails are located on the south shore, ranging in length from 1.5-miles to six miles. Details for these hikes may be picked up at the visitor center near South Lake Tahoe.

You'll find 11 trails located on the west shore ranging in length from three-quarters of a mile to six miles. The north and east shores each have six hiking trails. We explored Hidden Beach Trail up to Tunnel Creek Station. This trailhead is located 1.5-miles north of Sand Harbor State Park on Highway 28. However, parking was difficult and the trailhead isn't marked. When the trail guide tells you this is one to save for a cooler day, believe it. There is very little shade along this steep road, but you do get some great views of the lake below you.

Runners interested in racing can obtain information on the Lake Tahoe Race Series from Northstar: 916-587-0280.

D.L. BLISS STATE PARK
LAKE TAHOE

LOCATION - This park is on the southwest side of Lake Tahoe between Meeks Bay and Emerald Bay.

ACTIVITIES - Camp in one of 168 campsites. Reservations: 916-525-7277.

You can also picnic, fish, swim and tour the visitor center. Food is available. Enjoy the sandy beach at Rubicon Point near Emerald Bay.

Hikers can take the half-mile Balancing Rock self-guided trail, or walk over to the lake's only lighthouse, three-quarters of a mile away. Hike the Rubicon Trail which follows the shoreline for three miles to the mouth of Emerald Bay. Then, if desired, you can continue another two miles to reach Vikingsholm. Rubicon Point is the deepest section of the lake where the water drops to a depth of 1,400 feet.

INFORMATION -
D.L. Bliss State Park
916-525-7277
    or
Tahoe National Forest Headquarters
Highway 49 and Coyote Street
Nevada City, California 95959
916-265-4531

EMERALD BAY STATE PARK
LAKE TAHOE

Emerald Bay provides a good view of Fannette Island, where you can see a tea house sitting on top of the hill, which was built for Mrs. Lora Knight, who also had Vikingsholm Castle constructed. To tour the castle from mid-June through Labor Day, hike down the mile-long trail from the Emerald Bay overlook. Guided tours begin on the half hour from 10-4. A fee is charged.

The park opens May 27, and its campground has 100 sites. To make reservations, call 916-541-3030. Besides camping, you can also swim and go fishing.

INFORMATION -
Emerald Bay State Park
916-541-3030 (summers only)
    or
Tahoe National Forest Headquarters
Highway 49 and Coyote Street
Nevada City, California 95959
916-265-4531

SUGAR PINE POINT STATE PARK
LAKE TAHOE

LOCATION - Nine miles south of Tahoe City.

ACTIVITIES - Picnic, camp, tour the nature center, swim or ride the bicycle trail that begins here and continues north to Tahoe City. Hike the Sugar Pine Point Nature and Lighthouse Trail to see the only operating lighthouse on the lake. A short nature trail gives you the history of Lake Tahoe.

The Ehrman Mansion is open for tours. The original log cabin built here by the old Indian fighter, General Phipps, was used as the setting for part of the filming for the motion picture "The Godfather II."

INFORMATION -
Sugar Pine Point State Park
916-525-7982
    or
Tahoe National Forest Headquarters
Highway 49 and Coyote Street
Nevada City, California 95959
916-265-4531

DONNER LAKE STATE PARK
39

LOCATION - The park is on Donner Pass off U.S. I-80 at the Donner Lake exit.

FEATURES - This is where the Donner party became stranded without food during the winter of 1846. They built several crude cabins in an effort to survive, but out of the original 89, only 47 survived the ordeal.

ACTIVITIES - Try your endurance skills in the Donner Lake Triathlon which involves a 6.9-mile run around the lake, a half-mile swim in the lake and a 15-mile ride up to the summit of Donner Pass. Information: 916-587-2754.

The park opens in late May, when you can also enjoy picnicking, camping, hiking, fishing, water skiing, swimming and boating. For campground reservations, call 916-587-3841. A museum is open from 10-4 with exhibits explaining the story behind the ill-fated Donner travelers. Stop by Emigrant Monument.

Take a glider ride from the Truckee Airport. For information: 916-587-6702.

INFORMATION -
Donner Lake State Park
916-587-3841

or
Tahoe National Forest Headquarters
Highway 49 and Coyote Street
Nevada City, California 95959
916-265-531

GROVER HOT SPRINGS STATE PARK
40

LOCATION - The park is in Hot Springs Valley at 6,000 feet, three miles west of Markleville on California 1. Because of its elevation, temperatures should be quite pleasant during the summer months.

ACTIVITIES - The park has 76 campsites, hiking trails, fishing and two concrete pools fed by the hot springs. The pools are open from 9-9, seven days a week. A fee is charged.

INFORMATION -
Grover Hot Springs State Park
916-694-2248
     or
% Calaveras Big Trees State Park
P.O. Box 120
Arnold, California 95223
209-532-0150

MOUNT SAN JACINTO WILDERNESS STATE PARK
41

LOCATION - From the center of Palm Springs, follow California 111 north to Palm Canyon. Turn left onto Tram Drive and drive up approximately 2,000 feet to park and catch the tram. It's on the world's largest single span lift, rising from the floor of Chino Canyon to an elevation of 8,516 feet. As you ascend, you get some magnificent views since you can see all the way from Mount San Gorgonio to the Salton Sea. An early start is recommended since the trams fill up quickly.

The tram operates from October through Labor Day, and in 1988, cost $12.95 for adults. You can call ahead to get their schedule of special activities: 916-325-1391. An Alpine Restaurant is on top.

ACTIVITIES - Camping is available in backpacking or equestrian sites for which a permit is required. You can also enjoy picnicking, or hiking.

A nearby attraction is a 40-mile drive up Rim of the World Drive, California 18, to Lake Arrowhead. You'll reach elevations of 5,000 to 7,000 feet.

INFORMATION -
Mount San Jacinto Wilderness State Park
P.O. Box 308
Idyllwild, California 92349
714-659-2607

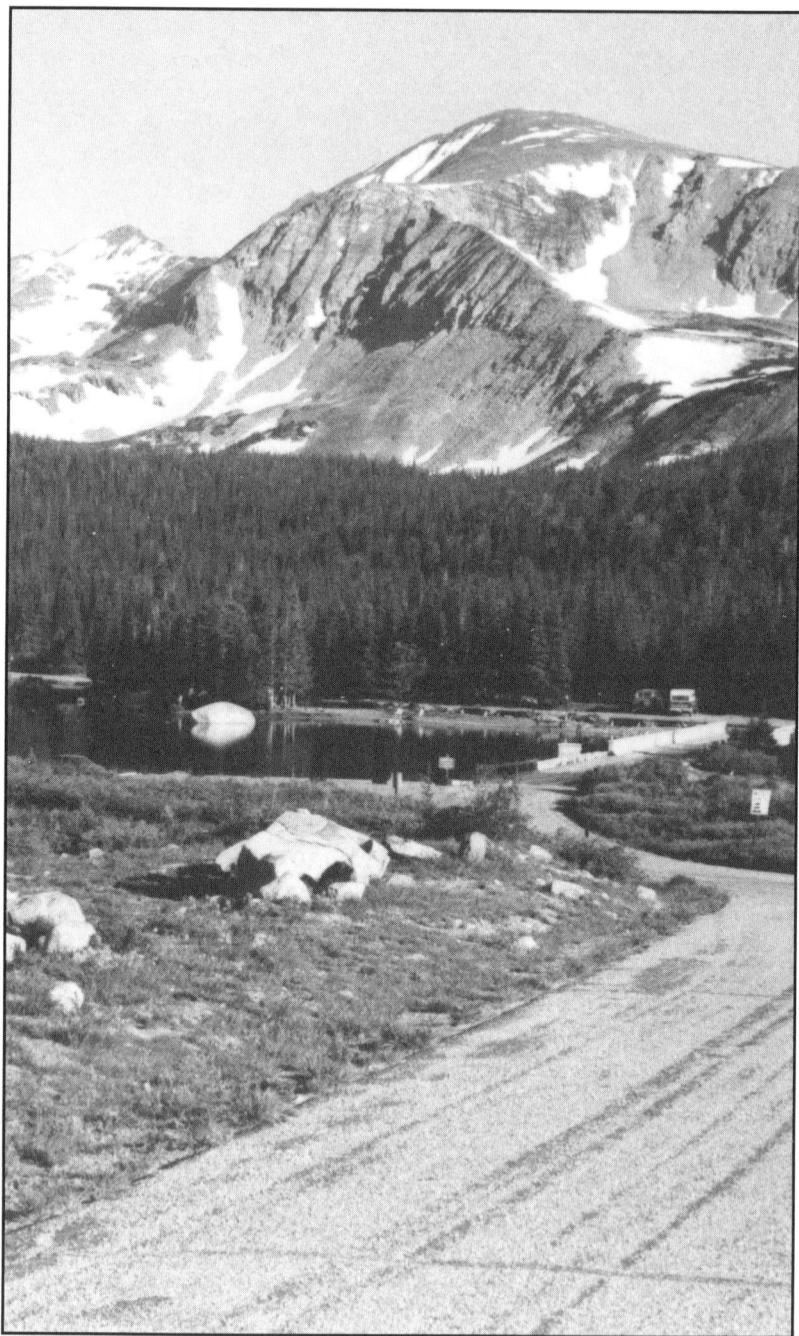

Colorado's mountains offer many recreational activities.

WALTER R. BORNEMAN

COLORADO

The state has 27 state parks ranging from beautiful lakes and reservoirs located near Denver along the Front Range to others situated high in the cool Colorado mountains. Visitors will find park activities geared primarily for summertime enjoyment. For campground reservations, contact Mistix at 303-671-4500, 9-6 Monday-Saturday and 9-3 Sunday.

BARR LAKE STATE PARK
1

LOCATION - Drive northeast from Denver on I-76 to Bromley Lane. Turn east on Picadilly Road and drive south to reach the park entrance.

ACTIVITIES - The park is for day use only. The closest campground is opposite the park on I-76. Picnicking facilities are available and horseback riders can ride along park trails.

Go fishing from a rowboat, sailing, canoeing and windsurfing. Swimming, diving,wading and powered boats are not permitted.

A nine-mile trail circles the lake. If you hike the three-mile round-trip along the southern boardwalk from the nature center, you'll reach a gazebo where you can get a great look at the heronry at the south end of the lake. Three hundred species of birds have been spotted here and a network of boardwalks and trails enable the visitor to get a good look at the lake's animal inhabitants. Guided nature walks are available. Check at the visitor center for a schedule or call 303-659-1160.

INFORMATION -
Barr Lake State Park
13401 Picadilly Road
Brighton, Colorado 80601
303-659-6005 (park)
303-659-1160 (nature center)

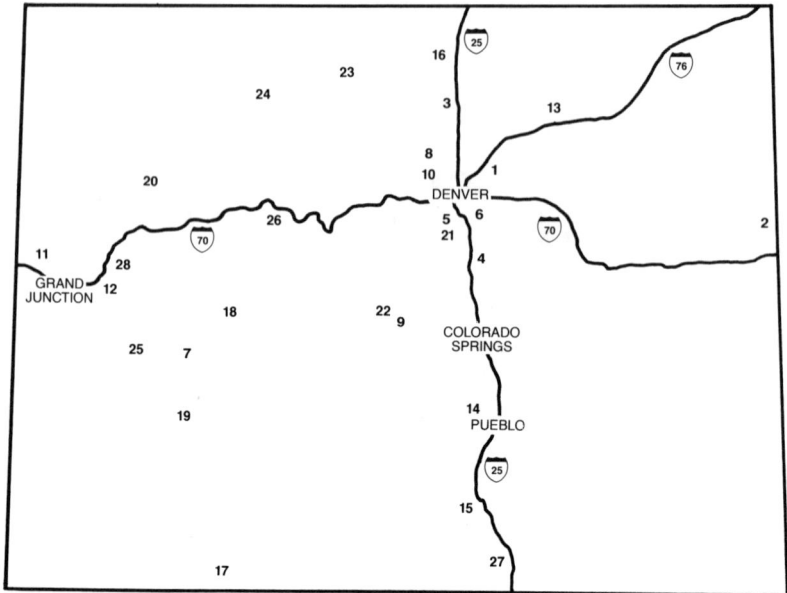

16

25

24

23

3

13

76

8
10

1

20

DENVER

26

6

2

70

5
21

70

11

28

4

GRAND
JUNCTION

12

18

22
9

COLORADO
SPRINGS

25

7

19

14

PUEBLO

25

15

17

27

BONNY STATE RECREATION AREA
2

LOCATION - Drive 23 miles north of Burlington on Colorado 385, and then turn east on County Road 2 and 3. The lake is located 1.5 miles east of the highway.

ACTIVITIES - The lake has sandy beaches from which you can go swimming and water skiing in warm water. You can also go sailing or fishing for a wide variety of fish. Since the lake is ringed with cottonwoods, camping in one of its 210 campsites is well shaded. Holding tank dump stations are located at Wagonwheel and Foster Grove campgrounds.

The Bonny Marina has boat rentals, fishing tackle, gas and food available. Information: 303-354-7339.

In Burlington, stop by to see the Kit Carson County Carousel located at the county fairgrounds. Originally built in 1905, it has been lovingly restored and now operates from 6-8 on Saturday and Sunday evenings during the summer and during the county fair the first week in August.

INFORMATION -
Bonny State Recreation Area
3010 County Road 3
Box 78-A
Idalia, Colorado 80735
303-354-7306
Marina: 303-354-7339

BOYD LAKE STATE RECREATION AREA
3

LOCATION - The park is one mile east of Loveland. Follow U.S. 34 west of I-25, turning north on Madison Avenue, and then watch for signs directing you to the park.

ACTIVITIES - The park is one of the most complete outdoor recreation areas in northern Colorado thanks to funds from the state lottery. Visitors will find a white sand beach, solar-powered bath house, a new campground with 148 sites, and a marina with boat rentals, fuel, snacks, boating and fishing equipment. Food and drink are sold at Burger Bay. You can also play volleyball and have access to two playgrounds and two boat ramps, including a large ramp for sailboats located north of the main marina area.

The two-mile long lake offers waterskiing on the south side of the lake which is where the power boats go. The north end of the lake is favored by sailboats and sailboarders. Sailboarding lessons and rentals are available at the Outpost Sunsport in the north parking lot.

Fishermen can try their luck at catching walleye, bass, catfish and crappie.

A variety of regattas are offered during the summer. Watch for dates of annual hydroplane races, or try your luck at fishing for walleye during the spring.

Hike around Heinricy Lake located south of the campground

INFORMATION -

Boyd Lake State Recreation Area
3720 North County Road 11-C
 Loveland, Colorado 80537
303-669-1739
Marina: 303-354-7339

CASTLEWOOD CANYON STATE PARK
4

LOCATION - Drive 30 miles south of Denver on Colorado 83 to Franktown. Turn west on Colorado 86 and travel one-quarter mile to Douglas County Road 51. Turn south and go approximately three more miles to the park entrance.

Upon leaving the park, it might be advisable to retrace your route instead of driving through the park and continuing on to Parker, which is a longer route and is mainly on an improved dirt road.

FEATURES - This small park, at 6,000 feet, is only two miles long, but has some very pretty canyons and a waterfall located by one of the picnic areas. It's located below the ruins of the Castlewood Canyon Dam, built in 1890 for irrigation purposes. The dam collapsed in 1933 and caused a flood which resulted in a million dollars worth of damage.

ACTIVITIES - The park has 1.5-miles of hiking trails, several picnic areas and a rock climbing area. It's open for day use only.

INFORMATION -

Castlewood Canyon State Park
P.O. Box 504
Franktown, Colorado 80116
303-688-5242 or 303-973-3959

CHATFIELD STATE RECREATION AREA
5

LOCATION - The recreation area is south of Denver on Wadsworth Boulevard past County Line Road, C-470. Turn west into the Deer Creek Entrance, or go south on Santa Fe Drive to Titan Road, turn west and go to Roxborough Road, then north to reach the park entrance.

ACTIVITIES - This is an excellent site for all water activities, horseback riding along 24 miles of trails on the park's west side, bicycle riding or hiking along 18 miles of trails, or camping in one of 153 sites. A heron rookery is on the lake, and this is the only state park with a balloon launching area located at the Montgolfier Launch Site near the Deer Creek entrance.

The lake also has good fishing for trout, bass, catfish and other species.

INFORMATION -
Chatfield State Recreation Area
11500 North Roxborough Park Road
Littleton, Colorado 80125
303-797-3986
Marina: 303-794-8505
Livery: 303-978-9898

CHERRY CREEK STATE RECREATION AREA
6

LOCATION - The park is southeast of Denver. Take I-25 south until it intersects I-225 at Parker Road. The park is one mile south of I-225 on Parker Road.

ACTIVITIES - Because of its close proximity to Denver, this is a very popular park and on weekends it is filled to capacity by 10 A.M. Later arrivals have to wait until someone leaves. The park has water-based activities including fishing, swimming from a guarded beach during the summer, eight miles of hiking and biking trails, camping in 102 sites and 10 miles of trails for horseback riding.

You can rent mountain bikes from Bikes-To-Go located next to Smoky Hill Shelter near the swim beach. Bicyclists can ride horse trails on the west side of the park. A recently completed 2.8-mile trail links the area to Denver's Highline Canal Trail.

A shooting range and model airplane field with asphalt runways is located in the southwest end of the park. For further information, call 303-693-1765.

Many special events such as bicycling, foot races and sail regattas also occur

in the park. For information, call 303-690-1211.
INFORMATION -
Cherry Creek State Recreation Area
4201 South Parker Road
Aurora, Colorado 80014
303-690-1166
Marina: 303-770-3354
Stables: 303-690-8235
Cherry Creek Gun Club: 303-693-1765

CRAWFORD STATE RECREATION AREA
7

LOCATION - From Delta, take Colorado 92 to Hotchkiss. Stay right on 92, and drive 10 miles to Crawford. The park is one more mile further south.

ACTIVITIES - The park is at 6,600 feet and has 60 camp sites. There is a holding tank dump station in the center campground.

You can enjoy picnicking, boating, waterskiing, scuba diving and swimming in a roped off swimming area. The lake is known for its catfish, perch, rainbow and German brown trout. Use of minnows or fish for bait is prohibited.

Four miles east of Crawford, you'll see Needle Rock which towers 800 feet above the valley floor. There's a nature trail to explore here.

If you take Colorado 92 down to its intersection with U.S. 50, crossing the bridge at the east end of Curecanti National Recreational Area, you'll enjoy one of the more scenic drives in the state. If you're looking for a hike along the Gunnison River in the Curecanti area, take the first right-hand turn once you turn west onto U.S. 50. Walk down the stairs to the trail. This area also offers numerous boating, fishing, camping and picnicking opportunities.

INFORMATION -
Crawford State Recreation Area
P.O. Box 147
Crawford, Colorado 81415
303-921-5721

ELDORADO CANYON STATE PARK
8

LOCATION - This rock climbers' mecca is eight miles southwest of Boulder. Follow Colorado 93 south to Colorado 170. Turn west and continue through the town of Eldorado Springs to reach the park.

ACTIVITIES - This park is famous for its sheer rock walls which attract climbers from all over the country. It also has a couple of hiking trails, with a shorter hike of 1.9 miles leading to some old hotel ruins and a great overlook of the Continental Divide. A longer hike goes to the Walker Ranch, 4.5-miles away and involves a 1,500-foot elevation gain.

Bring along your swimming suit in the summer to enjoy a dip in the Eldorado Springs pool. You can also enjoy picnicking in the area.

Runners should watch for the race generally held in the early evening in early August as the sun sets behind the Flatirons. Following this four-mile race, you can cool off in the pool.

INFORMATION -
Eldorado Canyon State Park
Box B
Eldorado Springs, Colorado 80025

ELEVEN MILE STATE RECREATION AREA
9

LOCATION - The park is west of Colorado Springs. Take U.S. 24 west for 38 miles to Lake George. One mile west of the lake, turn left on County Road 92 and continue for 10 more miles.

ACTIVITIES - The park is one of the best to fish for trout, crayfish, pike, carp or crawdad. You can also camp by the water in one of 300 sites which may be reserved by calling 303-671-4500, or in one of 25 primitive campsites located in the backcountry at the east end of the reservoir. You can also take a 1.5-mile hike, fly your model airplane in a three-mile area or attend an evening program in the amphitheater at the North Shore Campground. Call 719-748-3401 for information.

The islands are off limits to visitors. The Denver Water Board owns the reservoir and doesn't allow swimming, waterskiing, or any water-body contact activities. Windsurfing is permitted, however, providing either a full wet suit or drysuit is worn. Boating is allowed from a half-hour before sunrise to a half-hour after sunset.

Nearby, visit Florissant Fossil Beds National Monument which has one of the best fossil beds in the world.

Southeast of Florissant is Dome Rock State Wildlife Area. The rock for which the area is named is quite similar to Yosemite's Half Dome.

INFORMATION -
Eleven Mile State Recreation Area

Star Route 2, Box 4229
Lake George, Colorado 80827
719-748-3401

GOLDEN GATE STATE PARK
10

LOCATION - To reach the park from Denver, take I-70 west to the Colorado 58 exit. Go five miles west to Washington Avenue, the Golden exit. Turn right on Washington Avenue and go 1.5-miles and then turn left on the Golden Gate Canyon Road. It's 15 miles to the visitor center. To reach the park from Boulder, drive south on Colorado 93 to the Golden Gate Canyon Road.

FEATURES - The park has some old cabins, forested terrain, and ranges in elevation from 7,600 feet to 10,400 feet.

ACTIVITIES - You can camp in one of 106 sites in the Reverend Ridge Campground, or in one of 35 tent sites in Aspen Meadows Campground in the north central section of the park. Horse campers have their own campsite at Deer Creek, while backpackers have access to 23 backcountry sites.

You can also picnic, attend an evening campfire program or hike the wide variety of trails in the area. For a description of what's available, either contact the visitor center or get a copy of my hiking guide, *Hiking Trails of the Boulder Mountains and Plains.*

Fishing is permitted in the streams and ponds in the park with the exception of the Visitor Center Show Pond. Ralston Creek and three of the other ponds are stocked with trout. A license is required.

Bicyclists will find a real challenge in cycling up the very steep hill to the Reverend Ridge Campground.

Nearby attractions include Central City, a mining town located six miles south of the park and often referred to as "the richest square mile on earth." Great quantities of gold were mined here in the late 1800s. Now the city offers mine tours, an opera house where performances are given during the summer, rustic saloons with western-flavored music and many Victorian houses. The jeep roads west of town will give you some exciting places to explore as well.

INFORMATION -
Golden Gate Canyon State Park
Route C, Box 280
Golden, Colorado 80403
303-592-1502

HIGHLINE STATE RECREATION AREA
11

LOCATION - The park is 14 miles west of Grand Junction. Take I-70 to the Loma Exit, or County Road 193. Turn north and go six miles to Q Road. Turn west and continue 1.2 miles to 11.8 Road. Then go north for one more mile to the park entrance.

ACTIVITIES - Camp in the campground with 25 sites, have a picnic, waterski, go swimming from the beach, boating or rubber tubing. There are two boat launching ramps. Fishing for trout in the fall is offered in the north end of the lake, while the warm water provides good catfish and crappie fishing.

Because of its popularity, the park can only handle 45 cars. Once it's full, new arrivals have to wait for someone to leave.

Colorado National Monument is four miles west of Grand Junction. Visitors can drive the 22-mile Rim Rock Drive to get a good view of the monument's geological formations such as Balanced Rock, Coke Ovens or Window Rock. Camping is available at Saddlehorn. You can also picnic, hike one of the trails or attend a summer evening program.

INFORMATION -
Highline State Recreation Area
1800 11.8 Road
Loma, Colorado 81524
303-858-7208

ISLAND ACRES STATE RECREATION AREA
12

LOCATION - The area is five miles east of Palisade and 17 miles northeast of Grand Junction. Take Exit 47 off I-70.

ACTIVITIES - The campground has 32 sites, an unguarded swimming beach, wakeless boating and fishing.

INFORMATION -
Island Acres State Recreation Area
P.O. Box B
Palisade, Colorado 81526
303-464-0548

JACKSON LAKE STATE RECREATION AREA
13

LOCATION - The lake is 80 miles northeast of Denver and 20 miles northwest of Fort Morgan. Take I-76 east and then turn north on County Road 39. Follow this road for 7.5-miles, passing through Goodrich. Then go west on YS, a paved road, for 2.5 more miles.

ACTIVITIES - Enjoy boating, waterskiing, camping in one of the 200 sites, swimming from two unguarded beaches and fishing for walleye, bass, catfish, perch, crappie and drum. The water in the sandy-bottomed lake is unusually warm for a Colorado lake. Since the water is used for irrigation, it may be low later in the summer.

Jackson Lake Sports has food, windsurfing lessons, boat rentals, supplies and fishing tackle. The park headquarters' amphitheater is the scene of weekend interpretive programs during the summer.

INFORMATION -
Jackson Lake State Recreation Area
263603 County Road 3
Orchard, Colorado 80649
303-645-2551
Boat Rentals: 303-288-2270

LAKE PUEBLO STATE RECREATION AREA
14

LOCATION - The park is located eight miles west of Pueblo on Colorado 96. Take the U.S. 50 West Exit from I-25, and then turn left on McCullough Boulevard to reach the Pueblo Reservoir turnoff.

ACTIVITIES - The lake has 60 miles of shoreline. You can enjoy swimming in the Rock Canyon Swimming Complex, go sailboarding or sailing, with sailboat and fishing boat rentals available at the concession stand on the north shore. Tour the visitor center on the south shore. Fishing is best during the spring.

You can also picnic, hike, horseback ride, fly model planes or scuba dive. The campground has 214 sites. Bikers can follow the 15-mile paved bikepath that goes around the lake, or ride the bikepath into town. You can rent bikes at the Pueblo Nature Center located three miles below the dam. Concessions are available at the marina. The park is quite busy on the weekends.

By 1990, plans have been made to build a natural amphitheater where outdoor musical dramas will be presented. They're scheduled to run Monday through Saturday during the summer.

In Pueblo, attend the Colorado State Fair held from the end of August into September or walk through the Fred E. Weisbrod Aircraft Museum adjacent to the Pueblo Airport. The museum contains over 20 fighter planes from World War II, plus modernistic high-speed rail equipment.

Take a raft trip down Rock Canyon on the Arkansas River with Adventure Bound, Inc. For information, call 719-544-8113.

INFORMATION -
Lake Pueblo State Recreation Area
640 Pueblo Reservoir Road
Pueblo, Colorado 81005
719-561-9320
North Marina: 719-547-3880
South Marina: 719-561-4000

LATHROP STATE PARK
15

LOCATION - The park is three miles west of Walsenburg on U.S. 160 on the north side of the road.

ACTIVITIES - The park is bordered by the Spanish Peaks on the south and the Sangre de Cristo Range on the west. It has two lakes where you can enjoy fishing, sailing, windsurfing, swimming and waterskiing.

One-hundred campsites with reservations are available through Mistix. Enjoy two-miles of hiking trails and four-miles for bicycling plus a nine-hole golf course.

For arriving light plane pilots, Johnson Field north of Walsenburg has two runways, one paved and the other grass.

INFORMATION -
Lathrop State Park
P.O. Box 111
Walsenburg, Colorado 81089
303-738-2376

LORY STATE PARK
16

LOCATION - The park is on the edge of Horsetooth Reservoir northwest of Fort Collins. Take U.S. 287 north through LaPorte. At the Bellvue exit, turn left. Drive one mile to County Road 23. Then turn left and go 1.4-miles to County Road 25G. Turn right and drive another 1.6-miles.

ACTIVITIES - The park is located near a lake surrounded with red sandstone rock walls and has a small camping area with seven sites. You can go boating either in the lake or on Horsetooth Reservoir which also offers waterskiing and sailboarding. There are 30 miles of hiking trails here plus 25 miles provided for horseback riding. For a guided horseback ride, contact the Double Diamond Stables at 303-224-4200.

The trails are also great for mountain biking or mountain running, for those of you who enjoy getting away from the city pavement.

INFORMATION -
Lory State Park
708 Lodgepole Drive
Bellvue, Colorado 80512
303-493-1623
Horseback riding: 303-224-4200

NAVAJO STATE RECREATION AREA
17

LOCATION - Follow U.S. 160 west out of Pagosa Springs for 17 miles. Then go southwest on County Road 151 for 18 miles to Arboles. Go another two miles south on County Road 982.

ACTIVITIES - Navajo offers 90 campsites, 2.5-miles of hiking trails, and fishing, for which a license is required.

INFORMATION -
Navajo State Recreation Area
Box 1697
Arboles, Colorado 81121-1697
303-883-2208

PAONIA STATE RECREATION AREA
18

LOCATION - Take Colorado 82 out of Glenwood Springs south to Carbondale. Take Colorado 133 over McClure Pass for 36 miles to reach Paonia Reservoir.

ACTIVITIES - The campground has 31 sites available, but you'll need to provide your own water. You can also go boating or sailing from the boat launch and fishing for trout and pike. The lake is popular for waterskiing because of its length.

Attend the Paonia Cherry Day Festival in July.

INFORMATION -
Paonia State Recreation Area
% Crawford State Recreation Area
P.O. Box 147
Crawford, Colorado 81415
303-921-5721

RIDGWAY STATE RECREATION AREA
19

LOCATION - The park is five miles north of Ridgway off U.S. 550, 20 miles south of Montrose and 12 miles from Ouray.

ACTIVITIES - The park was still under construction in 1988, but is scheduled for partial completion by 1989. It will have four recreation areas: Dutch Charlie opens in 1989 and will have a marina, beach, hiking trails and two campgrounds; Dallas Day Use opens in 1990 and will have hiking trails, picnicking and fishing; San Juan Overlook is scheduled to open in 1992 and will have hiking trails and a small picnic area. Pa-Co-Chu-Puk (Cow Creek), now scheduled to open in 1991, will have a group picnic area, hiking trails and stream fishing.

The reservoir is five miles long and a mile wide, and will offer water activities including motor boating, waterskiing, sail boarding, sailing, swimming, fishing and scuba diving. You can also go camping, picnicking, hiking, bicycling and horseback riding.

Nearby activities include a scenic drive from Ridgway along the old river road and railroad bed to Ouray. Access in Ouray is at the intersection of Oak Street and 7th Avenue. Turn right at the 4J Trailer Court.

West of Ridgway on Colorado 62, take the south turnoff onto the East Dallas Creek road. Drive seven miles to Willow Swamps for some good fishing near the base of Mount Sneffels. Another option is to go two miles north of Ridgway to Owl Creek Pass Road and drive east past Chimney Peak and Silverjack Reservoir, 20 miles away.

At the western edge of Ridgway are roads that go to Elk Meadows, Pleasant Valley and Loghill Village. These roads are negotiable by passenger car; however, it's advisable to check on local road conditions prior to attempting any backcountry driving.

Drive to Ouray, often referred to as the "Switzerland of Colorado." This town, nestled below towering red rock walls, offers beautiful hiking, swimming in a hot springs pool, touring Box Canyon where Canyon Creek disappears and reappears to drop 285 feet, and jeeping over Imogene Pass, Engineer Pass or Ophir Pass. You can rent jeeps in town through Jeeps Ouray: 303-325-4444 or 303-325-4154 or from Switzerland of America: 303-325-4484.

Mountain runners can test their endurance by running over Imogene Pass from Ouray to Telluride. This challenging 18-mile race climbs 4,000 feet before dropping 5,000 feet down into Telluride and is held the Saturday after Labor Day.

For a spectacular 23-mile drive, drive over the Million Dollar Highway from Ouray to Silverton, where over a billion dollars worth of minerals has been mined. The highway was constructed of mine tailings containing gold and silver from the local mines and it's said that the road contains a million dollars worth of these precious metals. There are many ghost towns along the route to this mountain mining town where you can enjoy lunch or stay overnight. Kendall Mountain in Silverton is the site of another annual mountain race held each July.

Silverton is also the terminal for the only 100% coal-fired, steam-powered, narrow gauge railroad operated in the U.S. The train runs between Durango and Silverton, and if you catch the train from Durango, you can return to Durango either by train or bus. Advance reservations are very necessary: 303-247-2733. Most tourists catch the train from Durango, but you can take a bus from Silverton to Durango and return to Silverton by train from early June through the end of August. For Silverton departures, call 303-387-5416.

One mile south of Montrose, tour the Colorado Historical Society's Ute Indian Museum.

INFORMATION -
Ridgway State Recreation Area
Ridgway Design Office
1332 East Oak Grove Road
Montrose, Colorado 81301
303-249-7983

RIFLE GAP STATE RECREATION AREA AND RIFLE FALLS STATE PARK
20

LOCATION - To reach the park, take I-70 to the Rifle interchange. Then follow Colorado 13, passing through Rifle. After three miles, take County Road

325 for 9.8 miles to reach the recreation area and then continue another five miles to reach the park.

FEATURES - There's a small herd of buffalo at the northwest end of the park and ice caves north of Rifle Falls.

ACTIVITIES - The recreation area offers 46 campsites, while the park only has 18. If you're lucky, you can camp next to a waterfall. A holding tank dump station is located at the entrance to Cottonwood Campground.

You can swim from an unguarded beach at the recreation area, waterski, sail, jeep around Cedar Mountain and enjoy hiking two miles of trails in the park. Crystal clear water and underwater rock formations have made the park one of the best for scuba diving in the state. You can fish for rainbow and German brown trout, walleye and bass.

A nearby attraction is Harvey Gap Reservoir east of Rifle Gap, a favorite for windsurfers and sailboaters. Large power boats are forbidden on the reservoir.

Pilots can land at the Garfield County Airport, three miles east of Rifle, where the 6,000-foot runway is paved. Rental cars are available at the airport from Budget: 303-625-3706.

INFORMATION -
Rifle Gap State Recreation Area and Rifle Falls State Park
0500 County Road 219
Rifle, Colorado 81650
303-625-1607

ROXBOROUGH STATE PARK
21

LOCATION - The park is southwest of Denver. To reach it, take U.S. 85, Santa Fe Drive, south to Titan Road. Turn right and drive 3.5-more miles. Remain on Titan and turn left to continue three more miles. The park entrance is on your left.

ACTIVITIES - The park, known for its red Fountain Formation, which is similar to that found in Red Rocks and Garden of the Gods, has twelve miles of hiking trails. It is managed for the preservation of its unique natural values and for such compatible activities as nature hikes, photography and birdwatching. Family pets, fires, camping and rock climbing are prohibited for this reason.

If you hike the Fountain Valley trail, you'll follow a 2.25-mile loop that winds through the Fountain and Lyons rock formations. Willow Creek Trail is a one-mile loop, South Rim Trail is three miles in length, and the trail to Carpenter Peak is 5.5 miles long and involves moderate to steep hiking.

INFORMATION -
Roxborough State Park
4751 North Roxborough Drive
Littleton, Colorado 80125
303-973-3959

SPINNEY MOUNTAIN STATE RECREATION AREA
22

LOCATION - Take U.S. 24 west out of Colorado Springs for 55 miles, crossing over Wilkerson Pass. Turn left on Park County Road 23 and go for 2.8-miles. Then turn right onto County Road 59 and continue 1.1-miles further to the park entrance.

ACTIVITIES - The area is open for day use only from May 1-November 15 from one-half hour before sunrise until one hour after sunset.

The area's main attraction is trophy fishing for cutthroat, rainbow and brown trout, northern pike and kokanee salmon. Fishermen can only use artificial flies and lures and can keep one trout measuring 20 inches or longer.

Visitors can also go boating, waterfowl hunting or have a picnic. Waterskiing and swimming are prohibited. The boat ramps are located on the north and south sides of the reservoir. Windsurfers are required to wear either a full wetsuit or a drysuit.

INFORMATION -
Spinney Mountain State Recreation Area
Star Route 2, Box 4229
Lake George, Colorado 80827-4229
303-748-3401

COLORADO STATE FOREST STATE PARK
23

LOCATION - The park is west of Fort Collins. Take Colorado Highway 14 for 75 miles, crossing over Cameron Pass. The park stretches along the western side of the Medicine Bow Mountains into the northern end of the Never Summer Mountain Range with elevations ranging from 8,500 feet to 12,500 feet. The roads inside the park are gravel.

The park itself is quite extensive, with two of the campgrounds located along Colorado 14 on Cameron Pass and east of the park headquarters.

ACTIVITIES - The park has 104 campsites at Ranger Lakes, The Crags, North Michigan Reservoir and Bochman. A dump station is located at the Ranger Lakes parking lot. Backcountry camping is available at Ruby Jewel,

Kelly, Clear and American lakes. Six rustic cabins with woodburning stoves, bunkbeds and mattresses are available for rent on the shore of the North Michigan Reservoir. For reservations, contact Mistix at 303-671-4500 or 1-800-365-CAMP.

A KOA Campground is located outside the entrance to the park. Reservations: 303-723-4310.

The park also has three yurts: accommodations constructed with waterproof walls and roofs, solid wood floors, bunk beds for six and complete with cooking utensils. For reservations: Never Summer Nordic, P.O. Box 1254, Fort Collins, Colorado, 80522, 303-484-3903. Mountain bike trail maps are also available from this group or at the park headquarters.

Four-wheelers will enjoy the many roads in the area such as the sand dunes located in the northeast part of North Park. The park contains Colorado's only moose herd.

The park allows only wakeless boating activities on North Michigan Reservoir. Fishermen can fish for brook, brown, native, rainbow and golden trout. Golden trout and grayling are found in Kelly Lake.

Hiking trails go to Ruby Jewel, Kelly, Clear, Agnes and American lakes. The park has 50 miles of hiking trails and 100 more miles for roaming about in the backcountry on horseback.

Red Feather Lakes are northeast of Walden where you can take summer pack trips, horseback rides out of the State Forest or enjoy guided fishing trips. Guides may be contacted by calling 303-723-4204 in Walden.

INFORMATION -
Colorado State Forest State Park
Star Route, Box 91
Walden, Colorado 80480
303-723-8366

STEAMBOAT LAKE STATE RECREATION AREA AND PEARL LAKE STATE PARK
24

LOCATION - Take U.S. 40 west from Steamboat Springs for two miles to County Road 129, the road to the airport. Turn north and continue 26 more miles to the Steamboat Lake Park entrance. Pearl Lake's entrance is three miles south of the turnoff to Steamboat Lake. To reach Pearl Lake, turn right at the well-marked intersection and drive east on a gravel road for two miles.

ACTIVITIES - The two parks have 200 campsites, and, since the parks are at 8,000 feet, offer cool summer weather. A holding tank dump station is located at Sage Flats by Steamboat Lake.

Picnic areas include Sage Flats, Placer Cove, Rainbow Ridge, Meadow Point, Dutch Hill and Pearl Lake.

You can hike half-mile Tombstone Trail, which begins at Placer Cove by Steamboat Lake or strike out into the surrounding mountains.

Go fishing in the clear water for rainbow trout in Steamboat Lake and for cutthroat trout in Pearl Lake. Sailing is also good here, especially on a summer afternoon when the winds often pick up.

Waterskiing and swimming are permitted only in designated areas in Steamboat Lake. Boat rentals are available at the concession stand at Dutch Hill Campground.

Pearl Lake permits only wakeless boating activities and has small craft rentals. While here, you can also go hiking, fishing and horseback riding.

Mountain biking would be also be fun to do along the roads in either of the parks.

Groceries are sold a mile south of Steamboat Lake at Hahn's Peak General Store which also has a restaurant and a guest ranch, or in Clark, south of the park.

Some beautiful hiking is also available in the Mount Zirkel Wilderness. To reach this site, watch for the Glen Eden Ranch, southeast of Lake Steamboat. Turn right onto Seedhouse Road and drive to the Slavonia parking area, approximately 12 miles away. One special hike is to Gilpin Lake, 4.5-miles, or you can follow the Mica Lake Trail above timberline.

Mountain climbers can go up Mount Zirkel, reached by hiking along the ridge above Gilpin Lake, or climb Big Agnes, reached from Mica Lake. For guides to these and other hikes, call Rocky Mountain Ventures at 303-879-4857.

Another scenic hike is up Hahns Peak. The road to the trailhead is east of The road to Steamboat Lake State Park. Watch for the marked turnoff to the right.

INFORMATION -
Steamboat Lake State Recreation Area and Pearl Lake State Park
Box 750
Clark, Colorado 80428
303-879-3922
Marina: 303-879-7019

SWEITZER LAKE STATE RECREATION AREA
25

LOCATION - The park is three miles west of Delta off U.S. 50 on E Road.

ACTIVITIES - Enjoy water activities including waterskiing, warm water fishing, boating, swimming from an unguarded but roped off beach, innertubing with a rental tube, wind surfing or snacking from their concession stand. The picnic areas are covered and line the edge of the beach.

INFORMATION -
Sweitzer Lake State Recreation Area
1735 E Road
Delta, Colorado 81416

SYLVAN LAKE STATE RECREATION AREA
26

LOCATION - Take I-70 to the Eagle exit. Travel south through Eagle on Main Street to the West Brush Creek Road. Turn right and continue 15 miles to the park entrance. The first 10 miles are on an oiled road, but the last five are on a gravel road. If you happen to be traveling on a motorcycle as we were in 1988, this drive is not advisable.

ACTIVITIES - Enjoy fishing, camping and picnicking.

INFORMATION -
Sylvan Lake State Recreation Area
% Rifle Gap State Recreation Area
0050 Road 219
Rifle, Colorado 81650
303-625-1607

TRINIDAD STATE RECREATION AREA
27

LOCATION - The park is three miles west of Trinidad on Colorado 12.

ACTIVITIES - There are 62 campsites and reservations may be made by calling 303-671-4500.

The park has four miles of hiking trails including three nature trails that originate near the campground. The Carpios Cove Trail begins in the picnic area adjacent to the campground and provides access to the Trinidad Lake shoreline. Since the park joins the Panadero Ski Area, you have additional mountain terrain for hiking, backpacking, jeeping or climbing. The lake offers water sports and fishing.

Trinidad's restored Bloom House was originally built in 1882. Guided tours are offered during the summer from 10-4.

INFORMATION -
Trinidad State Recreation Area
R.R. #3, Box 360
Trinidad, Colorado 81082
303-846-6951

VEGA STATE RECREATION AREA
28

LOCATION - The park is northwest of Collbran. Exit I-70 south onto Colorado 65, and then go east on Colorado 330 passing through Collbran. It's 12 more miles to the park.

ACTIVITIES - The park is great for water activities such as boating, waterskiing, fishing, as well as for hiking or riding along the two miles of trails or for camping in one of 128 campsites. Since it's at 8,000 feet, it's cool in the summer.

INFORMATION -
Vega State Recreation Area
Box 186
Collbran, Colorado 81624
303-487-3407

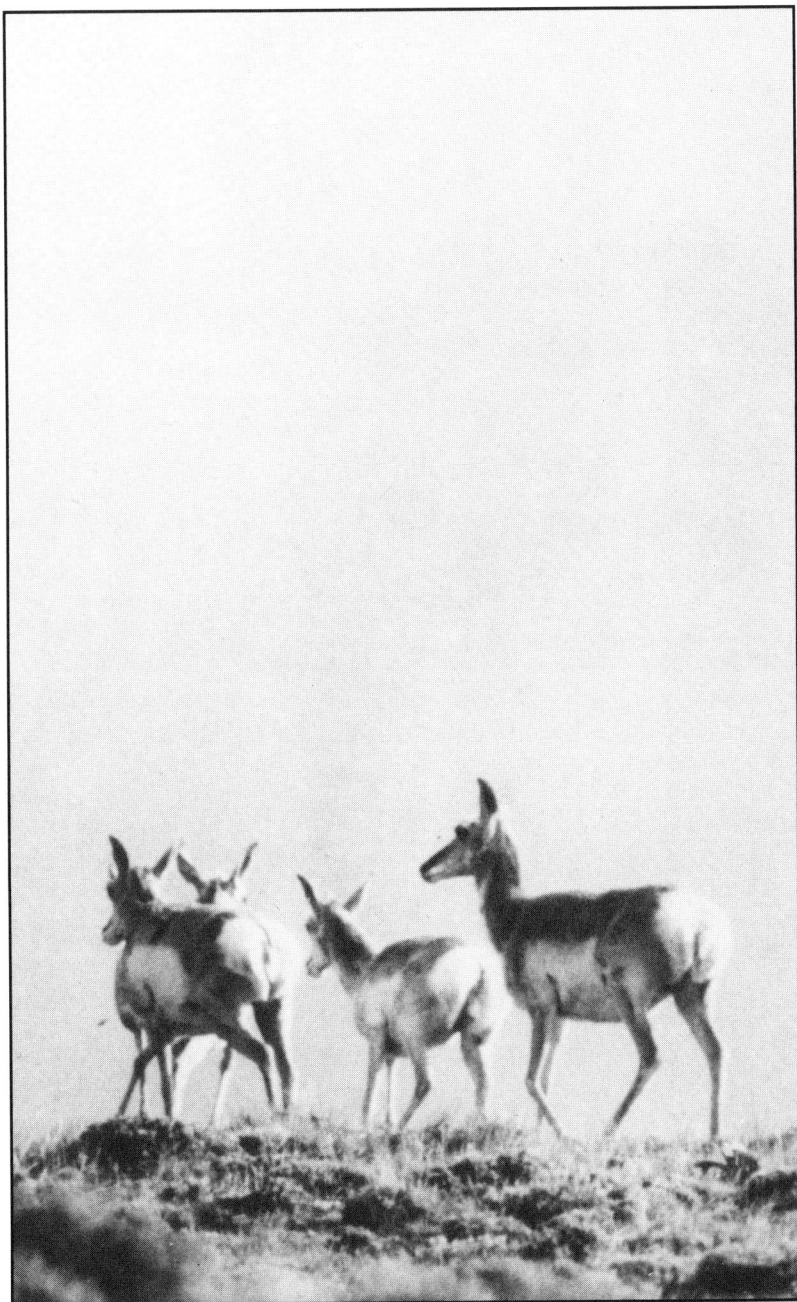

The American Pronghorn "antelope" are found in Colorado and Wyoming
in greater numbers than anywhere else in the world..

Morning clouds on Mauai.
WARREN DEHAAN

HAWAII

Visitors flying to the Hawaiian Islands are in for a real treat in terms of beauty and climate. Although there are actually more than 124 islands and small pieces of land rising above the ocean, most tourists only visit five of them: Kauai, Oahu, the Big Island, Maui and Molokai.

For more information for each individual state park, contact Division of State Parks, Department of Land and Natural Resources, 1151 Punchbowl Street, Honolulu, Hawaii 96813.

KAUAI - "THE GARDEN ISLE"

The island is the fourth largest of the Hawaiian islands and is 25 air miles from Honolulu. Kauai has the distinction of having the wettest spot on earth, Mount Waialeale, which rises 5,208 feet and receives between 400 and 600 inches of annual rainfall.

KOKEE STATE PARK
1

LOCATION - The park is at 3,600 feet and is adjacent to Waimea Canyon on the west side of Kauai. It's reached by driving up Waimea Canyon Drive from Waimea or by via Hawaii 550 from Kekaha.

FEATURES - Waimea Canyon is referred to as the "Grand Canyon of the Pacific," and when you see it, you'll discover why.

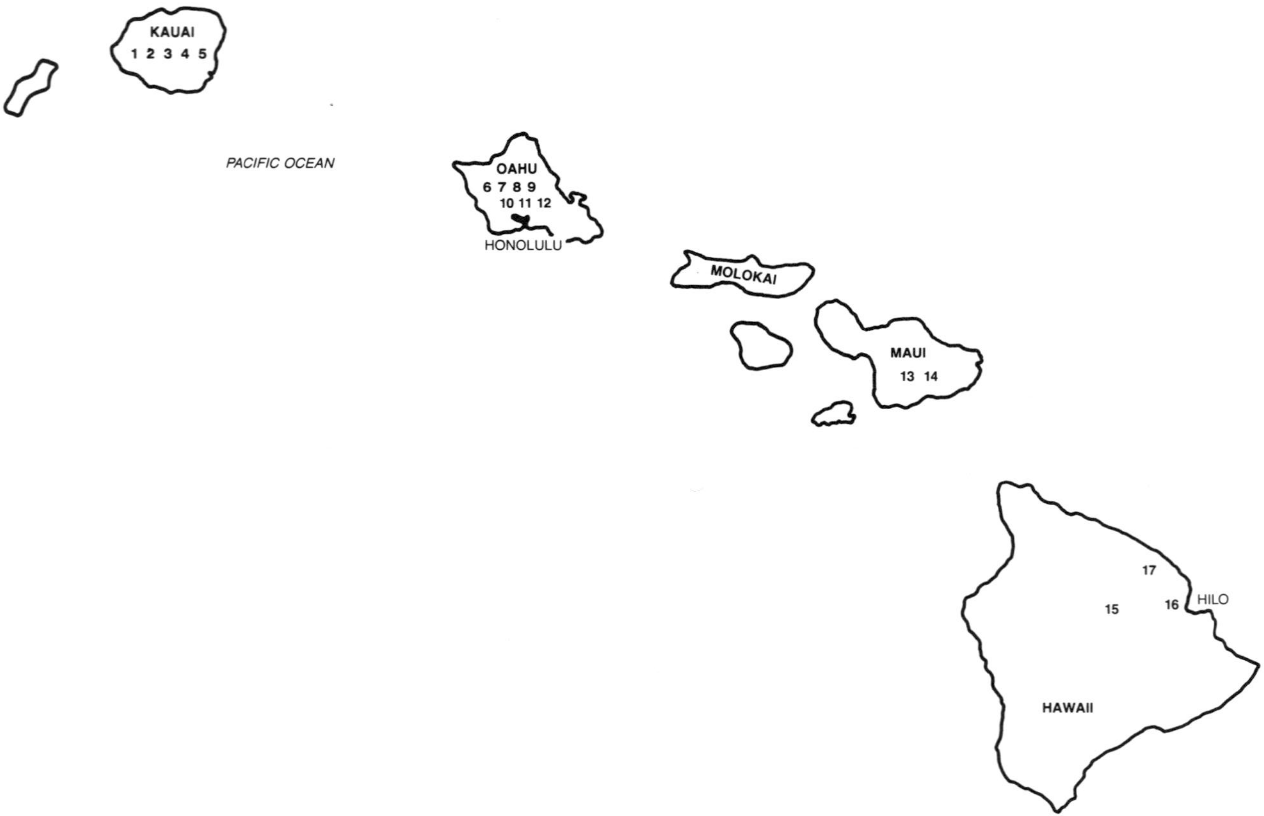

HILO

17

16

15

HAWAII

MAUI
13 14

MOLOKAI

OAHU
6 7 8 9
10 11 12

HONOLULU

PACIFIC OCEAN

KAUAI
1 2 3 4 5

ACTIVITIES - The park has picnic grounds, cabins, a campground with cold showers, pig hunting and trout fishing.

The literature lists 45 miles of hiking trails, but it's advisable to check at the park headquarters to be sure which ones are still accessible. When we hiked there in 1986, one of them had been closed by a hurricane and was totally impassable.

A couple of possibilities includes hiking the Cliff Trail, a .1-mile hike to Cliff Lookout where you can picnic at a table overlooking Waimea Canyon. Canyon Trail involves a 1.7-mile hike down to Kumuwela Lookout.

Tour the museum to see an exhibit on the plants and geology of the area. It's open from 10-4.

Be sure to continue through the park for four more miles to the Kalalau Lookout for a spectacular view of the valley and ocean below you, weather conditions permitting. A picnic area and restrooms are located here.

WAIMEA CANYON STATE PARK
2

LOCATION - The park is 11.1 miles north of Kekaha. Drive up the road leading to the Kokee State Park, Waimea Canyon Drive, Hawaii 550. The road winds and climbs, so be ready for some mountainous driving.

ACTIVITIES - At the 3,400-foot level, you reach Canyon Lookout, where you can see the deep gorges cut into the surrounding plateau and can easily understand why the area is often referred to as "The Little Grand Canyon."

Hike the short nature trail, or, if you're truly ambitious, you can take the long, difficult hike in and out of the canyon. The trail is located in the adjacent forest reserve.

HAENA STATE PARK
3

LOCATION - End of Kuhio Highway, Hawaii 56.

FEATURES - See the wet caves, ancient sea caves formed around 4,000 years ago. You can also see a dry cave with its opening on a cliff facing the beach. It's the large end of a lava tube whose smaller end is located on top of the cliff.

ACTIVITIES - This is a good spot for shore fishing and seeing the spectacular Na Pali Coast. Follow the short path at the end of the road which goes up to a former Hawaiian Hula temple where the youth once came to learn native chants and dances. Swim at Ke'e Beach.

NA PALI COAST STATE PARK
4

LOCATION - The park is located next to Haena State Park at the end of Hawaii 56.

ACTIVITIES - The trailhead for the 11-mile long Kalalau Trail begins here. This is a very difficult and demanding hike, and crosses high sea cliffs and beautiful valleys with magnificent waterfalls. The first half-mile will provide you with some great ocean views. After the first two miles, you come to Hanakapiai Valley Beach, where there is a primitive backpacking camp and beach. Swimming or wading here can be dangerous because of the rip tides.

The next campground is four miles further. This hike is quite strenuous along steep switchbacks as you climb up into the Hanakoa Valley. The last five miles eventually ends up at Kalalau Beach which is only usuable during the summer. Winter surf usually covers this area. Be sure to bring along plenty of insect repellent.

You can take a boat tour of the area. Tours are offered by Na Pali Kai Tours: 808-822-3553 or 808-826-9011. Depending upon the ocean conditions, you can snorkel or swim from the boat below cliffs which rise high above your head. Whale watching is popular from December-April.

Zodiac boats will also take you either on a tour of the area, or drop you off to camp at Kalalau Beach or at Miloii.

An even better way to see these spectacular cliffs is to take a helicopter ride. Check at the airport for rates and times. This ride also takes you over Mount Waialeale. You'll overfly gorges that are 3,000 feet deep and even drop into the crater itself.

INFORMATION -

Na Pali Coast State Park
Division of State Parks
3060 Eiwa Street
P.O. Box 1671
Lihue, Hawaii 96766
808-245-4444

WAILUA RIVER STATE PARK
5

LOCATION - The park is on the east side of the island along the banks of the Wailua River off Kuhio Highway, Hawaii 56.

ACTIVITIES - Take a riverboat cruise up the river to Fern Grotto. It begins from the Wailua River Marina, one-quarter of a mile west of Hawaii 56 on the south side of the river. The excursion takes approximately one and one-half hours, and passes the site of several sacred temples located along the river bluffs. Once in the grotto area, you'll hike through some thick vegetation where you're treated by your guides singing the "Hawaiian Wedding Song" in the natural amphitheater.

The park has six separate recreation areas to visit. If you drive to the Polishu area, two miles up Hawaii 580 and west of Hawaii 56, you can get a good view of the river and Opaekae Falls. Drive up to see Wailua Falls at the end of Maalo Road, Hawaii 583.

Enjoy sunbathing, swimming, picnicking and shore fishing at Lydgate State Park, across from the Wailua River State Park. The Wailua Beach Section offers opportunities for sunbathing, swimming, bodysurfing and board surfing.

OAHU

The island of Oahu is the third largest in the Hawaiian chain and the most populated. As you fly in, you'll pass Diamond Head. If your arrival is timed right, watch some incredible surfing on the Banzai Pipeline.

HANAUMA BAY STATE UNDERWATER PARK
6

LOCATION - Three-tenths of a mile east of Hawaii Kai off the Kalanianaole Highway, Hawaii 72.

FEATURES - The cove is the result of volcanic action that occurred 10,000 years ago.

ACTIVITIES - Buses run to the area from Waikiki, and another shuttle takes you down to the beach area if you decide not to walk down the steep hill. The shuttles run daily from 7-6. This is a great area for scuba diving or snorkeling within a protected cove. Locals bring along frozen peas to feed the resident fish.

KAENA POINT STATE PARK
7

LOCATION - The park is located at the end of Farrington Highway in Makua, Hawaii 930, along a remote coastline at the northwest tip of the island.

ACTIVITIES - Picnic and fish along the shoreline. Hike the 2.7-mile trail along the volcanic coast with its tide pools and stone arches. Watch for porpoise near the mouth of the stream if you're hiking early in the morning. There's a large sandy beach at Yokohama Bay, but only the experts enjoy body surfing and board surfing. During the summer the water is often calmer for swimming.

KAHANA VALLEY STATE PARK
8

LOCATION - The park is at 55-222 Kamehameha Highway, near Kahana on the east side of the island off Hawaii 83.

ACTIVITIES - See the Hiulua Fishpond or get a permit in advance to hike the 4.9-mile long trail. Picnic in the coconut grove or enjoy swimming and bodysurfing in nearby Kahana Bay Beach Park.

SACRED FALLS STATE PARK
9

LOCATION - One mile south of Hauula on the east side of the island off Hawaii 83.

ACTIVITIES - Hike two miles to the base of the 80-foot falls. The last section of the trail goes through a deep canyon. It's closed during rainy weather.

SAND ISLAND STATE PARK
10

LOCATION - The park is at the end of Sand Island Access Road off Nimitz Highway, Hawaii 92.

ACTIVITIES - Tent camping only with flush toilets and cold showers. You can also picnic, swim and fish from the shore and go board surfing.

DIAMOND HEAD STATE MONUMENT
11

LOCATION - The monument is off Diamond Head Road between Makapuu Avenue and 18th Avenue in Honolulu.

ACTIVITIES - The park is open for day use only. Diamond Head is Hawaii's most well-known monument and is a large tuff cone formed around 100,000 years ago by a series of explosive eruptions. Visitors can enjoy a picnic on the crater floor's meadow or hike .7-mile to get a panoramic view of Honolulu. Bring a flashlight along if you decide to hike.

WAIMANALO BAY STATE RECREATION AREA
12

LOCATION - The recreation area is on Kamahameha Highway, Hawaii 83, between Bellows Air Force Base and Aloiloi Street in Waimanalo.

ACTIVITIES - This park contains part of one of the state's largest sandy beaches where visitors can participate in board and body surfing, swimming, picnicking and camping in the ironwood grove.

MAUI - "THE VALLEY ISLE"

Haleakala is the high point on Maui, with its neighboring volcano, Puu Kukui, rising 10,023 feet.

IAO VALLEY STATE PARK
13

LOCATION - From Wailuku, drive out High Street, Hawaii 32, to reach the Iao Valley Road.

FEATURES - The valley is carved from a one-mile deep gorge. Here Kamehameha I trapped and destroyed the army of the king of Maui. The river flowing through the park is called the Kepaniwai, "damming of the waters," named for the many bodies of the Maui warriors which filled the water.

The needle itself rises 2,250 feet, and has been deeply eroded and covered with vegetation and is visible from Wailuku. It's especially beautiful to see in the late afternoon as the sun highlights the peak.

Watch for the rock profile of President Kennedy as you drive to the park. You'll see several cars parked at a bend of the road below the rock formation.

ACTIVITIES - Follow the paved trail along the stream to see the lush growth of the many rain forest plants. Swim in the small swimming holes in the river. Climb up the stairs to get a good overlook of the valley. There was even a wedding being held at the top of the stairs when we visited.

There are a couple of botanical gardens that are interesting to tour as you make your way up the valley. You can also stop by Kepanival Park to learn about the different groups of people who have settled on the island.

WAIANAPANAPA STATE PARK AND CAVES
KAUMAHINA STATE PARK
PUAA KAA STATE PARK
HOOKIPA STATE PARK
14

LOCATION - These state parks are located along the road to Hana, Hawaii 30, except for the caves which are 2.5-miles from Hana.

ACCESS - Hana is reached by driving a very winding road carved out of the rain forest. It's 52.8 miles from Kahalui to Hana, and you should allow a full day to drive there and back. The road has 56 one lane bridges, and tourists insist that it must have at least 900 curves, although there are only 617 of them. Be sure to have a full tank of gas before you leave Paia.

As you drive to Hana, stop by the Kaenae Arboretum to see many more tropical plants.

Kaumahina State Park is 25 miles from Kahului and offers some great views of the Hanomanu Bay and coastline.

Puaa Kaa State Park has freshwater pools and waterfalls, so bring along your swimsuit.

Hookipa State Park is known as the windsurfing capital of the world and is the site of many major international competitions.

You can't drive all the way around the island after reaching Hana unless you have a four-wheel-drive vehicle. During the rainy season, the roadbed serves as a streambed, so check with the park rangers at Ohe'o Gulch if you're planning to go the circle route.

If the drive sounds like too much of a challenge, you can fly into Hana on AlohaIslandAir. For information: 808-244-9071. Several of the helicopters that take you on flightseeing trips also fly into here. If you're a licensed pilot, you can also fly there yourself by chartering a light plane from the Kahalui Airport.

Wainapanapa Cave was formed inside an old lava tube, where the water sometimes turns to a bright red because of the very tiny red shrimp that live here. According to an old legend, however, the water is believed to be red from the blood of a Hawaiian princess who was killed here by her jealous husband. The "crying" sounds you hear here aren't her voice, but are the result of the water pouring through the opening in the tube.

The park is four miles from Hana and has one and one-half miles of trails you can explore in the rain forest, a black sand beach, and some old lava caves. You can camp here or stay in one of the cabins, but prior arrangements for camping must be made. Contact the Department of Land and Natural Resources in the State Office Building, 54 High Street, Wailuku. Free permits are issued which are good for up to five nights. Call 808-244-4354.

Be sure to have lodging reservations if you plan to stay overnight. You can purchase groceries at the well-known Hasegawa General Store or get a meal at the hotel. In Hana, see the century-old lava rock Wanalua Church.

Ten miles south of Hana at Kipahulu is Wailua Falls, scene of the film classic, "Mutiny on the Bounty." These "Seven Sacred Pools" pour into one another with waterfalls in between, and offer good swimming as well as great photography. Hike around in the bamboo forest to see some of Hawaii's rare birds and plants.

While in Maui, you should also plan to visit Haleakala National Park, "House of the Sun." It's a great place to watch either a sunrise or a sunset. For information on the viewing conditions and times, call 808-572-7749.

As you drive to the summit, stop at the Kalahuku Overlook to see the silversword plant which only grows here on the volcano. It can reach nine feet in height and only blooms once in its lifetime.

Fifteen-minute talks are given daily at 9:30, 10:30 and 11:30 A.M. at the summit house. Be sure to dress warmly since the weather conditions are variable, changing from sunny to windy and rainy in a few minutes.

Take the Crater Hike, a guided 2.5-mile descent via Sliding Sands Trail at 10:00 A.M. on Saturday, Sunday or Tuesday. Meet at the House of the Sun Visitor Center on the crater rim.

Take a birding walk in the forest reserve. Meet at the Hosmer Grove Campground Monday, Thursday and Friday at 9:00 A.M.

Enjoy a four-hour hike to Waimoku Falls and Makahiku Falls. Meet at the

Oheo Gulch parking lot outside of Hana on Saturday at 9:00 A.M.

Take a downhill bicycle ride from the summit of the crater at 10,023 feet to Paia on the coast. This is an all day ride, and you're picked up around 3:00 A.M. Suggestion: Do this upon your arrival before you've adjusted to Hawaiian time. The bicycles have "megabrakes". Contact either Cruiser Bob's: 808-667-7717 or Maui Downhill Bicycle Safaris at 808-871-2155.

In Lahaina, go to the Hyatt Regency Maui on Wednesday through Sunday at 8:00 or 9:00 P.M. to see their slide show on the constellations and look at deep space through their telescope.

"Flightsee" the neighboring islands. If you can't fly yourself in a rented lightplane as we did, be sure to take a chartered ride aboard either a fixed wing or a helicopter to see all the waterfalls along the north shore of Molokai, Maui and the Big Island. Also it's a great way to get to Hana and avoid the three or four hour drive.

The volcano on the Big Island was quite active in 1988, and if weather permits, you can get a great look at the lava pools and the lava flow covering the road as it flows into the ocean, sending up huge clouds of steam.

BIG ISLAND OF HAWAII

Most people visit the Big Island to see Kilauea Iki's lava flows. Since it's not as explosive as Mount St. Helens, you can watch the whole show from a safe vantage point. The Volcano House on the rim provides a great overlook of the caldera. If you can get a flight over the vent that was flowing in 1988, you'll see a huge billowing cloud of steam forming where the molten lava meets the sea.

MAUNA KEA STATE PARK
15

LOCATION - The park is on the flank of Mauna Kea in the Pohakiloa Area at 6,500 feet on Saddle Road, Hawaii 200. It's 35 miles west of Hilo. Before driving there, be sure to check with your car rental agency to see if they permit their cars to be taken there.

FEATURES - Located near a jagged rift in the mountain, the park is like an oasis with its spatter cones and cinder cone formations.

ACTIVITIES - Skiing is available from November through late January, weather permitting. You can enjoy a picnic or stay overnight here as well.

WAILUKU RIVER STATE PARK
16

LOCATION - The park is off Waianuenui Avenue in Hilo.

FEATURES - The park has several overlooks of the Wailuku River. Boiling Pots is at the end of Pepee Falls Drive, two miles from the center of town via Waianuenue Avenue. You can see several large pools which are connected by underground water system. You can hike along the trail in this area, but use caution.

To reach 80-foot Rainbow Falls, go west on Wainuenue Avenue. The falls come off a lava lip and fall into the basin below where you can see a rainbow formed from the mist in the morning. The falls diminish during the summer.

AKAKA FALLS STATE PARK
17

LOCATION - The park is at the end of Akaka Falls Road, Hawaii 220, on the east side of the island. It's 3.6 miles southwest of Honomu.

FEATURES - The park features two 400-foot waterfalls. They vary in width depending upon the amount of water in the Kolekole Stream that feeds it. Rainbows form when the sun hits the water's mist.

ACTIVITIES - Hike a .4-mile loop along a steep paved path to an overlook of the falls. The trail passes through much dense vegetation. Picnic facilities are available.

Massacre Rocks State Park and the Snake River.
BILL GRANGE, IDAHO PARKS & RECREATION

IDAHO

Idaho has 22 state parks and, interestingly enough, gold has been found in some form in almost every county in the state. The state's famous geyser near Soda Springs is the largest carbon dioxide gas geyser in the world. It shoots 175 feet high. Shoshone Falls on the Snake River near Twin Falls is even higher than Niagara falls, plunging 212 feet from its 1,000-foot channel.

Idaho is known as the whitewater capitol of America. For information on guided float trips, contact the Idaho Outfitters and Guides Association, P.O. Box 95, Boise, 83707, or call 208-342-1438.

BEAR LAKE STATE PARK
1

LOCATION - Eighteen miles south of Montpelier on U.S. 89.

ACTIVITIES - Both East and North Beach are day use areas suitable for swimming, fishing and boating. Some of the fish seen here are found nowhere else in the world and include "big Mac" mackinaw and the unique Bonneville Cisco that run in January.

INFORMATION -
Bear Lake State Park
P.O. Box 252
Paris, Idaho 83261
208-945-2325

BRUNEAU DUNES STATE PARK
2

LOCATION - Eight miles northeast of Bruneau off Idaho 51.

FEATURES - The dunes, which rise 470 feet, are North America's tallest

14

15

4

COEUR
D'ALENE

12

10

7   8

6

18

13

5

3 BOISE
17
9

2

16   10 84

84

11

POCATELLO

15

15

84

1

single structured sand dunes. These dunes are unique because they have been sculpted in the center of a natural basin rather than at its edge. For around 30,000 years, this natural trap has caused the sand to collect in this semi-circular basin. The dunes receive less than 10 inches of annual precipitation, and temperatures range from 110 degrees in the summer to below zero during the winter.

The park is part of the Snake River Birds of Prey Area where you can watch eagles and hawks soar overhead.

ACTIVITIES - Have a picnic, hike the Sand Dunes Trail, a five-mile trip for which a hiking path is available, or follow the one-third-mile self-guided nature trail.

Tour the information center, attend interpretive programs and camp in the campground which has 48 sites, 32 of them with hookups.

Since most of the park's inhabitants are nocturnal, the best time for spotting any wildlife is in the early morning or late evening. This is also the best time for taking pictures of the dunes.

The park has two lakes formed when the C. J. Strike Reservoir, located five miles from the dunes, was filled, causing the water table to rise. The lakes offer fishing for bluegill, bass and channel catfish from non-motorized boats and canoes. The largest lake also has a bouyed swimming area. The reservoir itself offers boating, fishing, swimming and camping as well.

A popular nearby attraction is the Bruneau Canyon Overlook, about 25 miles from the park via paved and gravel roads.

INFORMATION -
Bruneau Dunes State Park
Star Route B, Box 41
Mountain Home, Idaho 83647
208-366-7919

EAGLE ISLAND STATE PARK
3

LOCATION - Eight miles west of Boise. Follow Idaho 44 to Linder Road and then follow the signs.

ACTIVITIES - The park is open for day use only. It was formerly used as an honor farm for state prison inmates and has a swimming beach with its own bathhouse, waterslide, picnic and concession stand. Non-motorized boating is also permitted. You can fish only in the Boise River channels.

INFORMATION -
Eagle Island State Park

State House Mall
Boise, Idaho 83720
208-939-0696

FARRAGUT STATE PARK
4

LOCATION - This park, the second largest in Idaho, lies at the foot of the Coeur d'Alene and Bitterroot mountains. It borders Idaho's largest lake, Pend Oreille, and is located 23 miles north of Coeur d'Alene. To reach it, turn east off U.S. 95 from Athol. Drive four miles on Idaho 54 to the park's entrance.

ACTIVITIES - The park was originally the site of a large U.S. Naval Training Station during World War II and has rifle ranges, two amphitheaters, a model airplane flying field, camping facilities and the capacity for 500 people to picnic. Water and electrical hookups are provided in Snowberry Campground. Reservations: 208-683-2425.

The lake has 111 miles of shoreline and offers fishing for kokanee salmon, cutthroat, German and brown trout and perch. The largest bull trout in the world are native to the lake. The best time to fish for trophy-sized fish is in October and November. The fishing in May and June is adversely affected by the spring run-off. February and March are the best times to fish for kokanee.

Tour the park museum, go horseback riding or hiking. Rent a mountain bicycle and ride along the unused logging roads. A bath house is located at Beaver Bay's swimming area which accommodates 300 swimmers. Park naturalists present nightly programs during the summer.

Go boating or sailing. A boat launching ramp and dock are provided at the Eagle Marina. Gas, fishing and boating needs may be met at Bayview, the locale for the largest number of sailboats. Over 35 Lake Pend Orielle Yacht Club sailboat races are held here throughout the year. Concessions are available.

In late June, you can join the "Celebrate Summer" festivities with glider demonstrations, a fun run, bike races and the Pacific Northwest radio-controlled scale master's airplane championships.

In May, in Coeur d'Alene, a festival is celebrated with a boat parade, logging contest and a marathon run on Memorial Day weekend. From mid-June through the end of August, attend the Summer Theater presented by the Carrousel Players who offer nightly performances. Attend the Folk Festival and the Inland Empire Wooden Boat Show with classic boats on display in mid-July, and in early August, watch for the Chinook Derby and the Coeur d'Alene triathlon.

Take a boat cruise on Lake Coeur D'Alene, departing from the Coeur d'Alene

Resort downtown. The cruises leave at 1:30 and 5:00, from June through Labor Day, and last two hours. Information: 208-664-9241

North of the park, in nearby Bayview, are some old lime kilns erected in the early 1900s when limestone was being quarried.

Private aircraft can land at Athol Airport near Farragut on a 4,000-foot turf runway, or at the Henley Aerodome near Athol on a 4,300-foot paved runway.

Enjoy a scenic drive past Lake Coeur d'Alene along Idaho 97 on the east shoreline. The best views are from Exit 22 on I-90 at Wolf Lodge. Continue south for 38 miles to Harrison, watching for scenic markers along the route.

INFORMATION -
Farragut State Park
Box F
Athol, Idaho 83801
208-683-2425

HARRIMAN STATE PARK
5

LOCATION - Eighteen miles north of Ashton on US 20/191 and 33 miles southwest of Yellowstone Park.

ACTIVITIES - This day use only park offers fishing in a well-known fly fishing stream, Henry's Fork of the Snake River. In late July, attend the Snake River Regatta.

Photograph the rustic log cabins that were part of the historic "Railroad Ranch." You can also hike the trails, ride horseback, tour the information center and attend an interpretive program. Concessions are available.

No camping facilities are available, but visitors can reserve the rustic log dormitory facilities and the original Railroad Ranch Cookhouse.

INFORMATION -
Harriman State Park
Star Route, Box 33
Ashton, Idaho 83420
208-558-7368

HELLS GATE STATE PARK
6

LOCATION - Four miles south of Lewiston on Snake River Avenue, the park is 30 miles from the entrance to Hells Canyon National Recreation Area.

ACTIVITIES - Hells Canyon National Recreation Area itself has almost 1,000 miles of trails that traverse the area. They range from ones that are well maintained to some that are rarely touched. It's advisable to check with the park authorities prior to hiking.

The park is a departure point for a one to a five-day trip through to the famous Hells Canyon National Recreation Area, North America's deepest canyon, averaging 6,600 feet in depth. The canyon has whitewater rapids as well as deep pools. To schedule a float trip, whitewater rafting or boat tour, contact Hells Canyon Adventures for reservations: P.O. Box 159, Oxbow, Oregon 97840, or call 503-785-3352 in Oregon, or 800-422-3568 out of state. For a more complete listing of river tours and float trips, contact either the Chamber of Commerce in Clarkston at 208-758-7712 or in Lewiston at 208-743-3531.

In the park you can enjoy camping, picnicking, volleyball, boating, horseback riding and swimming. You can also fish for trout, bass and steelhead, or go hiking or biking. Snacks and groceries are available. The campground has hookups and a dumping station.

Joggers, bikers, fishermen and visitors interested in a fish viewing room with a fish ladder can go to Lewiston's Levee Parkway.

INFORMATION -
Hells Gate State Park
3620 A Snake River Avenue
Lewiston, Idaho 83501
208-743-2363

HENRYS LAKE STATE PARK
7

LOCATION - The lake is between Plummer and St. Maries on Idaho 5 south of Coeur D'Alene.

ACTIVITIES - Go fishing, boating, have a picnic, swim, hike the trails, tour the information center or attend interpretive programs. Snacks, groceries and lodging are available in the park.

In late May in St. Maries, the Old Timer's Picnic is held featuring old logging trucks, draft horses and various games.

INFORMATION -
Henrys Lake State Park
Summer Star Route, Box 20
Macks Inn, Idaho 83433
208-558-7532

HEYBURN STATE PARK
8

LOCATION - Near St. Maries on Idaho 5 on Lake Chatcolet.

ACTIVITIES - Camp in one of the sites near Benewah Lake or by Chatcolet Lake. Fishermen can cast for trout, bass or kokanee. Other lake activities include boating, waterskiing, sailing and canoeing.

Hiking and horseback riding trails are shaded by 400-year-old Ponderosa pines. The hiking trails range in length from a half mile to three miles. Indian Cliff Trail has a self-guiding booklet.

If you're here the second weekend in July, you'll be in time for the riverfest complete with log burling and a picnic. In early August, a new festival has been started: Wild Rice Festival. The Thursday before Labor Day, attend Paul Bunyan Days which features a lumberjack competition, antique auto show and a carnival.

Private pilots can land at St. Maries Municipal Airport on a 3,900-foot paved runway.

INFORMATION -
Heyburn State Park
Route 1, Box 139
Plummer, Idaho
208-686-1308

LUCKY PEAK STATE PARK
9

LOCATION - Ten miles southeast of Boise on Idaho 21.

ACTIVITIES - The park has three units. Sandy Point and Discovery Unit are for day use only. Discovery Unit is nine miles southeast of town and offers hiking, picnicking, fishing and swimming in the Boise River. Sandy Point is 10 miles southeast, or one mile beyond Discovery, and has fishing, picnicking and swimming from a guarded beach except on Wednesday and Thursday.

Spring Shores Unit is 16 miles southeast of town. Turn right after the Mores Creek Bridge and continue for one more mile. This unit has facilities for picnicking, boating and fishing.

INFORMATION -
Lucky Peak State Park
Statehouse Mall
Boise, Idaho 83720
208-344-0240

MALAD GORGE STATE PARK
10

LOCATION - I-84 Hagerman Exit 147, near Tuttle, and east of Bliss.

FEATURES - The 250-foot gorge was created by meltwater flowing from an alpine glacier. The water forms a 60-foot waterfall at Devil's Washbowl. Upstream from the Washbowl are very faint traces of the old Malad Way Station which served as a stopping point along the Kelton Road from 1869-1879.

ACTIVITIES - The park is open for day use where you can photograph the gorge, picnic, hike or attend an interpretive program. If you hike the trail along the gorge, watch for some of the old run-off water channels.

A nearby attraction is the Hagerman Valley section of the Snake River Canyon along Idaho 30. The area's best known for Thousand Springs cascading out of the canyon walls. Fisherman will enjoy fishing for trout in the Malad River or in Oster Lakes. The Snake River offers boating and rafting. Three hot springs resorts offer summertime swimming.

Motorcyclists have access to the Hagerman Fossil beds across the Snake River from Hagerman. Motorcycles can ride on 19 miles of roads. Fossils found here date back 3.5-million years.

INFORMATION -
Malad Gorge State Park
Route 1, Box 358
Hagerman, Idaho 83332
208-837-4505

MASSACRE AND REGISTER ROCKS STATE PARK
11

LOCATION - Twelve miles west of American Falls, take Exit 147 off I-84.

FEATURES - Massacre Rocks was named after an Indian skirmish on two pioneer immigrant trains traveling past here along the Oregon Trail in 1862. The wagon trains had to negotiate a narrow pass where travelers feared Indians might be waiting in ambush. The settlers weren't attacked in the park, but east of there, where ten lost their lives.

The Malad River makes a very sharp descent in the park, resulting in a series of waterfalls and a gorge 2.5-miles long.

ACTIVITIES - Go camping, fishing, boating, see Oregon Trail artifacts and visible trail ruts, tour the information center or attend an interpretive program. Evening programs are presented during the summer every night except Monday and Tuesday and begin at dusk. One of the activities offered in 1988 was a guided nature walk along the Snake River.

Register Rock is where some of the Oregon Trail immigrants scratched their names and is located two miles west of the campground. Take along a picnic and your horseshoes for pitching.

Boat docks are located 1.5-miles west of the campground. Experienced rock climbers will find good climbing opportunities here. Hike an easy two-mile trail that crosses a footbridge spanning the gorge above Devil's Washbowl.

In June, a special event includes the Black Powder Shoot and Trapper Rendezvous. Father's Day features a fishing derby and the Oregon Trail Motorcycle Fun Run. The third week in August, attend the county fair and rodeo; the fourth weekend in August, watch for the Indian Springs Treasure Hunt.

INFORMATION -
Massacre and Register Rocks State Park
HC 76, Box 1000
American Falls, Idaho 83211
208-548-2672

OLD MISSION STATE PARK
12

LOCATION - The park is located 27 miles east of Coeur d'Alene and 10 miles west of Kellogg on I-90 off Exit 39, one mile east of Cataldo.

FEATURES - The old mission, named for the restored Old Sacred Heart Mission, is Idaho's oldest standing building and was constructed by the Coeur d'Alene Indians between 1850 and 1853 under the supervision of Jesuit missionaries.

ACTIVITIES - Walk along the history and nature trails or request a tour of the restored mission church. Enjoy a picnic or attend an interpretive program. Each August 15, the Coeur d'Alene Indians return to the mission to celebrate the "Feast of the Assumption." Fishing is available nearby in the Coeur d'Alene River.

In mid-August, attend the district mining contest with jackleg drilling, timber spiking and handmucking. Also the second weekend in August features the Miner's Day Picnic — a ten-day celebration.

INFORMATION -
Old Mission State Park
P.O. Box 135
Cataldo, Idaho 83810
208-682-3814

PONDEROSA STATE PARK
13

LOCATION - Two miles northeast of McCall on East Lake Drive to the forested peninsula on the east side of Payette Lake.

ACTIVITIES - Ponderosa Park has 170 campsites with reservable sites, some with water only, and others with both water and electricity. There are 62 other units without either water or electricity.

The Lionhead State Park Unit is located on the north tip of the lake and is the departure point for boats headed to Upper Priest Lake, which has a quarter-mile white sand beach and a primitive campground with 47 sites. Enjoy hiking to Lionhead Falls and be sure to bring along a swim suit for dipping in the pool at the bottom of the waterfall.

The Squaw Bay Campground is 23 miles north of Coolin and has spaces for 12 RVs. A cabin there sleeps eight. Make reservations through Priest Lake State Park: 208-443-2200.

The Dickensheet Unit has 11 sites in its campground and is a popular entry point for rafting and canoeing down Priest River. It's also a good spot for trout fishing.

The Indian Creek State Park Unit offers a large sandy beach, camping in 92 sites with some set up to accommodate RVs. Here you can go boating, waterskiing, hiking or enjoy a picnic. A hiking booklet of the area is available. One possibility for a hike is to go to Hunt Lake.

There are several additional hiking possibilities near McCall. Contact the McCall Chamber of Commerce at Box D, or call 208-634-7631.

INFORMATION -
Ponderosa State Park
P.O. Box A
McCall, Idaho 83638
208-634-2164

PRIEST LAKE STATE PARK
14

LOCATION - Thirty-five miles north of Priest River, follow the signs off Idaho 57.

FEATURES - Priest Lake is 19 miles long and is connected to Upper Priest Lake by a two and one-half-mile river called Thoroughfare. The lake is really divided into two lakes, and is surrounded by 80 miles of shoreline with sandy beaches. The lake is at 2,434 feet and summer temperatures average 75 degrees.

Water temperatures are also in the 70s during the summer.

ACTIVITIES - Enjoy fishing, picnicking, swimming, boating, horseback riding and camping near the lake. You can also hike well-marked trails, watching for the huckleberries when they're in season in August, and attend the interpretive programs. Snacks and groceries are available.

The area has two landing strips. Coolin is on the east side near Cavanaugh Bay and has a 3,400-foot gravel runway, and Priest Lake is at Nordman with a 3,850-foot turf runway.

To do some boating or river floating, contact the Priest Lake Guide Service, Star Route, Box 134, Nordman, Idaho 83848, 208-443-2357; or the Priest River Float Trip, P.O. Box 715, Priest River, Idaho 83856, 208-448-2813.

On Memorial Day weekend, attend the Priest Lake Spring Festival and flotilla cruise, fishing derby, catamaran regatta and the golf classic. The second weekend in August features the Huckleberry Festival. In mid-September, check out the Mushroom Festival at Priest Lake.

The U.S. Forest Service owns the majority of the property on the west side of the lake where there are five additional campgrounds along the lower lake and two boating/hiking campgrounds accessible on Upper Priest Lake.

The lake also has a number of water resorts, restaurants, boat, canoe, catamaran and windsurfing rentals, golf, tennis, swimming and waterskiing. Fishing guides are available.

INFORMATION -
Priest Lake State Park
Indian Creek Bay #423
Coolin, Idaho 83821
208-443-2200

ROUND LAKE STATE PARK
15

LOCATION - Ten miles south of Sandpoint off U.S. 95, then two miles west on Duford Road. It's also 36 miles north of Coeur d'Alene and then two miles west on Dufort Road north of Westmond.

ACTIVITIES - The lake itself is relatively shallow, only measuring 37 feet at its deepest section. Enjoy swimming, fishing, picnicking, touring the information center and hiking. If you walk around the lake, you'll be treated to two miles of shade under a canopy of trees.

You can also go skin diving and boating, but motorboats are prohibited. The campground has 53 campsites, but none have hookups. The sites are all shaded by large evergreens.

A fishing derby is held the first Sunday in May. In late May, a Waterfest is held, complete with racing and other water activities.

The town of Sandpoint is located on the western shore of Lake Pend Oreille, and this lake also provides opportunities to sail, windsurf, waterski, swim, dive and fish for "world class fish." The marina is on East Lake Street, one block from Main: 208-263-1493.

During the summer, the town sponsors an artwalk, a self-guided walking tour of the art galleries and businesses in town where art exhibitions are on display.

In early July, attend the Panhandle Rodeo in Sandpoint. The fourth weekend in July features a Bluegrass festival, while the first and second weeks in August offer a festival, "Symphony under the Stars." A variety of musical concerts are presented in Sandpoint from the end of July through mid-August. For information on the Festival at Sandpoint: 208-265-4554.

Aircraft can land at the Sandpoint Municipal Airport on a 3,980-foot surfaced runway.

INFORMATION -
Round Lake State Park
P.O. Box 170
Sagle, Idaho 83860
208-263-3489

THREE ISLAND CROSSING STATE PARK
16

LOCATION - Off I-84 at Glenns Ferry.

FEATURES - This historical park is a monument to the emigrants who, in the 1800s, were traveling west to the Oregon Territory. They had to cross the Snake River, and many who crossed here had a difficult time. If they chose not to cross at this point, they faced a longer and more difficult route along the south side of the Snake River. In 1869, Gus Glenn put in a ferry a short distance above the crossing, and you can still see ruts left behind by the wagon trains south of the ferry departure point.

Summertime temperatures range between 60-80 degrees, and Glenns Ferry is often referred to as Idaho's "Banana Belt" because of its mild winters and warm summers.

ACTIVITIES - The park has 50 campsites with electricity and hookups. A day use area is located along the banks of the Snake River with a picnic shelter that can be reserved. Hike a half-mile interpretive trail to learn more about the Oregon Trail. Fish for trout, bass, catfish, carp and sturgeon in the

Snake River.

Tour the visitor center where interpretive programs are offered during the summer. The park also offers swimming, bird watching, and a reenactment in August of the river crossing, using a horse and wagon. A 10-acre enclosed pasture holds five buffalo and two longhorn steers.

In early August, attend the county fair and rodeo.

INFORMATION -
Three Island Crossing State Park
P.O. Box 609
Glenns Ferry, Idaho 83623
208-366-2394

VETERANS MEMORIAL STATE PARK
17

LOCATION - The park is in Boise on State Street and Stilson Road.

ACTIVITIES - The park itself is a typical city park with picnic facilities, surfaced paths and an outdoor program area. The park adjoins Boise Lake and River.

INFORMATION -
Veterans Memorial State Park
960 Veterans Way
Boise, Idaho 83703
208-384-2812

WINCHESTER LAKE STATE PARK
18

LOCATION - One mile southwest of Winchester on U.S. 95.

ACTIVITIES - Go fishing, camping, picnicking, hike the trails or tour the information center where interpretive programs are presented.

INFORMATION -
Winchester Lake State Park
Winchester, Idaho 83555
208-924-7563

*Lewis and Clark Caverns are concealed in the rugged foothills
of the Tobacco Root Mountains in southeastern Montana.*

MONTANA

Montana is often referred to as "Big Sky" country, and it's easy to see why. Probably best known for its two national parks, Glacier and part of Yellowstone, the state has some very scenic lakes and rivers set aside for visitors to explore. The state parks offer both recreational as well as historical exhibits.

BANNACK STATE PARK
1

LOCATION - Five miles south of Dillon on I-15, 21 miles west on Secondary 278, and then four miles south on County Road.

ACTIVITIES - The park is the site of Montana's first major gold discovery in 1862. Take a walk and tour the ghost town which served as Montana's first territorial capital for one year. See Sheriff Henry Plummer's Gallows and the Meade Hotel.

At the time of the gold rush, the population numbered over 3,000, but the boom only lasted one year before the miners moved on to Alder Gulch 70 miles east.

Tour Bachelor's Row where the miners built more permanent shelters to protect them from the cold weather.

The visitor center and campground are open from mid-May through September.

On the last weekend in July, attend Bannack Days, a two-day event featuring frontier crafts, music, drama, black powder muzzle loader shooting, plus horse and buggy rides.

In June, the U.S. Open Fiddlers Contest is held in Dillon, and in August, the All-Girl Rodeo is presented.

INFORMATION -
Bannack State Park
P.O. Box 67

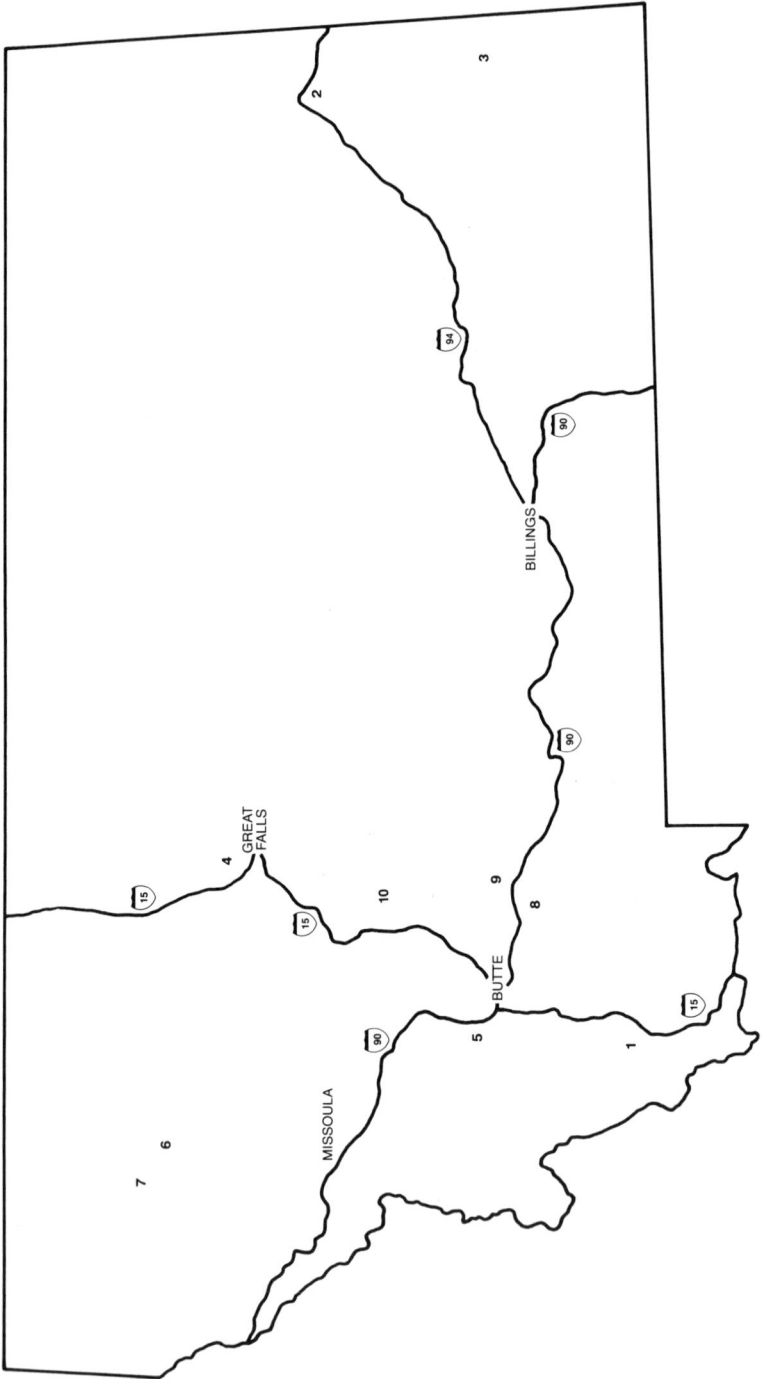

Kalispell, Montana 59903
406-834-3413

MAKOSHIKA STATE PARK
2

LOCATION - The park is three miles south of Glendive off U.S. 94. From Glendive, drive southwest on Merrill Avenue and turn left on Barry Street. Go under the railroad tracks, following Barry Street to Taylor Avenue. Turn right onto Taylor and then left onto Snyder Street to reach the park entrance.

FEATURES - The Indian word Makoshika means "bad earth," or "bad land." The rock layers here are even older than those found in the badlands of the Dakotas and have revealed fossils, which date back 65 million years, of over 10 species of dinosaurs and other creatures living during the "Age of Reptiles."

ACTIVITIES - See deeply eroded sandstone cliffs of the badlands which are especially beautiful at sunrise and sunset.

This park is a great place for rock hounds who enjoy searching for fossils and moss agates. To see an exhibit on the agates before you go hunting, stop by the Glendive Chamber of Commerce on North Merrill Avenue.

For a good view of the badlands, visitors can go hiking along Cap Rock, a .6-mile self-guided nature trail. This trail is three miles inside the park.

To go to the bottom of the badlands, hike the half-mile Kinney Coulee Trail, which descends 300 feet. To reach this trail, turn left at Radio Hill Junction and then take the first dirt road to the right. Hikers are urged to use caution since the badlands terrain is unstable and crumbly.

You can also camp, use their shooting range, or fish for a unique fish, a boneless paddlefish, which runs from May through early July.

The park has a 12-mile unpaved scenic drive that provides vistas of the terrain. Part of the road becomes impassable when wet and in places is very hilly and narrow. Trailers aren't allowed past the second mile because of the steep switchbacks and 15% grade.

Park naturalists are available for programs and tours. Contact them at 406-365-8596.

In mid-August, attend the four-day Dawson County Fair north of Glendive, which features country music, a rodeo and a tractor pull.

Dawson Community Airport is six miles to the south.

INFORMATION -
Makoshika State Park
R.R. 1, Box 2004

Miles City, Montana 95301
406-232-4375

MEDICINE ROCKS STATE PARK
3

LOCATION - Twenty-five miles south of Baker on Montana 7, milepost 10, then one-mile west on a county road.

ACTIVITIES - The park is the site where Indians once called up their magic spirits. See soft sandstone rock formations which look like Swiss cheese. The area is a wildlife haven and has camping and picnicking sites. In August, attend the Carter County fair and rodeo days.

INFORMATION -
Medicine Rocks State Park
R.R. 1, Box 2004
Miles City, Montana 95301
406-232-4365

GIANT SPRINGS HERITAGE STATE PARK
4

LOCATION - Follow U.S. 87 north through Great Falls, milepost 1.7, then go east three more miles on River Drive.

FEATURES - The park has one of the largest freshwater springs in the world and flows at the daily rate of 338 million gallons. It was discovered by the Lewis and Clark Expedition in 1805.

ACTIVITIES - The park is open for day use only when you can enjoy fishing, visit the nearby fish hatchery or picnic by the Missouri River.

East of the park, stop by Rainbow Falls and Dam at one of the two overlooks to see Horseshoe Falls, Crooked Falls and Rainbow Falls.

A nearby attraction, Ulm Pishkun State Park, a buffalo kill site, is located off I-15, 12 miles west of Great Falls. The area is almost a mile long and consists of a jumble of rock plus a sheer rock cliff face with small caves just large enough for a person to fit into. Indian paintings cover one of the cave's walls. Visitors can hike the interpretive trail, have a picnic or see the protected black-tailed prairie dog town.

In Great Falls, the state fair and rodeo with horse races is held in July.

Aeronautical buffs can tour the Malstrom Air Force Base Museum and Air Park located at the air base inside the main gate at the east end of Second

Avenue North. The outdoor park has aircraft and missiles which have been flown over the past 40 years. It's free and open from noon until 3:00 Monday through Friday, and on Saturdays during the summer. Information: 406-731-2705

Steam engine enthusiasts can tour the Mehmke Steam Museum located 10 miles east of town on U.S. 87/89 and see their collection of operable antique steam engines plus other farming artifacts. Information: 406-452-6571

INFORMATION -
Giant Springs Heritage State Park
P.O. Box 6609
Great Falls, Montana 59406
406-454-3441

LOST CREEK STATE PARK
5

LOCATION - One and one-half miles east of Anaconda on U.S. 10A, milepost five, then two miles north on Secondary 273, and six more miles west.

ACTIVITIES - The rock in the park is composed of tan colored granites, which were later cut through by glaciers that moved down the valley of Lost Creek around a million years ago. The grayish-green colored rocks were formed by the compacting and hardening of lime-rich muds which were deposited into the shallow sea that was here around 1.3 million years ago.

The park has 40 campsites. Hike over to see Lost Creek Falls, which drop 50 feet over a limestone cliff. Watch for mountain goats and bighorn sheep above the falls.

Anaconda is surrounded by one of the world's richest mineral deposits and is the site of an enormous copper mine where mining began in the 1880s. Only the smokestack remains, now the world's largest freestanding brick structure.

INFORMATION -
Lost Creek State Park
3201 Springer Road
Missoula, Montana 59801
406-542-5500

FLATHEAD LAKE STATE PARKS
6

WILD HORSE ISLAND STATE PARK
FLATHEAD LAKE STATE PARKS

LOCATION - Flathead Lake is located between Kalispell and Polson and is the largest body of fresh water in the west. It's 28 miles long and 15 miles wide at its broadest point. Access to the island is from Big Arm State Recreation Area via boat to Little Sheeko Bay from the northwest side of the island.

ACTIVITIES - The park is for day use only. You can enjoy fishing, hiking, boating and picnicking. Rental boats are available from commercial outfitters.

For a ride aboard a cruise ship, go eight miles south on U.S. 93 to the Vista Linda dock to ride aboard the Far West Cruise Ship. The boat departs at 2:00 P.M. daily from mid-June through September. Information: 406-857-3203 or 406-837-5569.

If you go to Polson, located at the foot of Flathead Lake, go to Riverside Park at the bridge to sign up for a half-day whitewater trip through a scenic canyon on the lower Flathead River. The Glacier Raft Company has departures at 10:00 A.M. and 2:00 P.M. from early June through early September. Reservations are encouraged: 406-883-5838 or 800-654-4359 inside Montana.

The Port Polson Princess gives one and one-half and three hour tours of Flathead Lake, departing at 10:30 A.M., 1:30, and 6:30 P.M. from early June through early September. Reservations: 406-883-2448.

INFORMATION -
Wild Horse Island State Park
P.O. Box 67
Kalispell, Montana 59903
406-752-5501

BIG ARM STATE PARK
FLATHEAD LAKE STATE PARKS

LOCATION - Twelve miles north of Polson on U.S. 93.

ACTIVITIES - The park has a long beach popular with swimmers and sunbathers. You can also camp, fish for lake trout, boardsail, scuba dive and waterski.

INFORMATION -
Big Arm State Park
P.O. 67
Kalispell, Montana 59903
406-849-5255 or 752-5501

ELMO STATE PARK
FLATHEAD LAKE STATE PARKS

LOCATION - Two miles north of Elmo on U.S. 93.
ACTIVITIES - The park is located on Big Arm, the largest bay on Flathead, and has a large, open campground with some junipers scattered about for shade. The campground is generally less crowded than others around the lake. You can go swimming, boardsailing or sailboating from its gravel shoreline.
INFORMATION -
Elmo State Park
P.O. 67
Kalispell, Montana 59903
406-849-5744 or 752-5501

FINLEY POINT STATE PARK
FLATHEAD LAKE STATE PARKS

LOCATION - This park is 11 miles north of Polson on Montana 35, and then four miles west on a county road.
ACTIVITIES - Fishing for lake trout and kokanee salmon is often excellent here.
INFORMATION -
Finley Point State Park
P.O. 67
Kalispell, Montana 59903
406-887-2715 or 752-5501

WAYFARERS STATE PARK
FLATHEAD LAKE STATE PARKS

LOCATION - The park is a half mile south of Bigfork on Montana 35 on the northeast shore of Flathead Lake.

ACTIVITIES - Go camping and picnicking in the forested campground. Enjoy taking nature walks along the shoreline to the nearby cliffs.

In May, Bigfork sponsors a whitewater festival on the Swan River for rafters and kayakers. Attend musical performances presented at the Summer Playhouse from late June through Labor Day.

INFORMATION -
Wayfarers State Park
P.O. 67
Kalispell, Montana 59903
406-837-4196 or 752-5501

WEST SHORE STATE PARK
7

LOCATION - Twenty miles south of Kalispell on U.S. 93.

ACTIVITIES - The campground has 30 campsites which are available from May 15 through September 15. Visitors can get some fantastic views of Flathead Lake as well as of the Swan and Mission mountains. Despite a rocky beach, enjoy boating and swimming.

INFORMATION -
West Shore State Park
P.O. 67
Kalispell, Montana 59903
406-844-3901 or 752-5501

LEWIS AND CLARK CAVERNS STATE PARK
8

LOCATION - Nineteen miles west of Three Forks on U.S. 10, or 47 miles east of Butte.

ACTIVITIES - You can camp here from June 15 through September 15. Tour the largest limestone caverns in the northwest. Take a two hour conducted guided tour offered daily from May 1-September 30.

Attend fireside chats in the campground during the summer, hike the self-guided trail, tour the visitor center, or have a snack in the cafe.

INFORMATION -
Lewis and Clark Caverns State Park
1400 South 19th

Bozeman, Montana 59715
406-287-3541 or 994-4042

MISSOURI HEADWATERS STATE PARK
9

LOCATION - Three miles east of Three Forks on U.S. 10 at the Three Forks Exit, east on Secondary 205 and then three more miles north on Secondary 286.

FEATURES - The park is the site where Lewis and Clark discovered that the Jefferson, Madison and Gallatin Rivers combined to form the Missouri River.

ACTIVITIES - Tour historic exhibits, enjoy camping from May 15 through September 15, picnicking, hiking the trails, fishing, river floating, and boating.

INFORMATION -
Missouri Headwaters State Park
1400 South 19th
Bozeman, Montana 59715
406-994-4042

CANYON FERRY STATE PARK
10

LOCATION - The reservoir is 10 miles east of Helena on U.S. 12/287 and then eight miles north on Montana 284.

ACTIVITIES - The reservoir has a 76-mile long shoreline and has three full-service marinas that can accommodate over 300 boats. Visitors can picnic, camp, go fishing or swimming.

Tour the visitor center at Canyon Ferry Village to learn about the dam's hydroelectric facilities.

INFORMATION -
Canyon Ferry State Park
P.O. 6609
Great Falls, Montana 6609
406-475-3060

Valley of Fire State Park.
VICI DEHAAN

NEVADA

Most visitors know about Las Vegas, but are unfamiliar with the great variety of state parks that are scattered throughout this state. Included here are some from three categories: scenic, historic and recreational. Most are open year-round, but may be closed due to bad weather during the winter.

BERLIN ICHTHYOSAUR STATE PARK
1

LOCATION - The park is near Gabbs on the western slopes of the Shoshone Mountains on Nevada 361.

FEATURES - The park contains the remains of Berlin, a typical 19th century mining camp, and has many old mining structures. Silver was mined here from the 1890s until 1909.

The other half of the park contains fossils of prehistoric fish-lizards called ichthyosaurs. These creatures were the largest animals of their day, 70 feet long, measuring eight feet around with ribs of nine feet. The animals resembled whales, had no gills and possibly weighed 40-60 tons. Thirty-four of them have been partially excavated, and a fossil display quarry with three others are on exhibit in the Fossil Shelter in Union Canyon, two miles from Berlin.

ACTIVITIES - Tour the Fossil House where an open pit displays the three fossils. Ranger talks are given daily at the Fossil Shelter from Memorial Day through Labor Day at 10:00 A.M., 2:00 and 4:00. The rest of the year, talks are given at the same times Thursday-Monday.

Tours of the townsite are given on Saturday and Sunday at 11:00 A.M. from Memorial Day through Labor Day.

Picnic or camp in one of 14 campsites from May through September. Hike the nature trail between Fossil Shelter and the campground.

INFORMATION -
Berlin Ichythosaur State Park

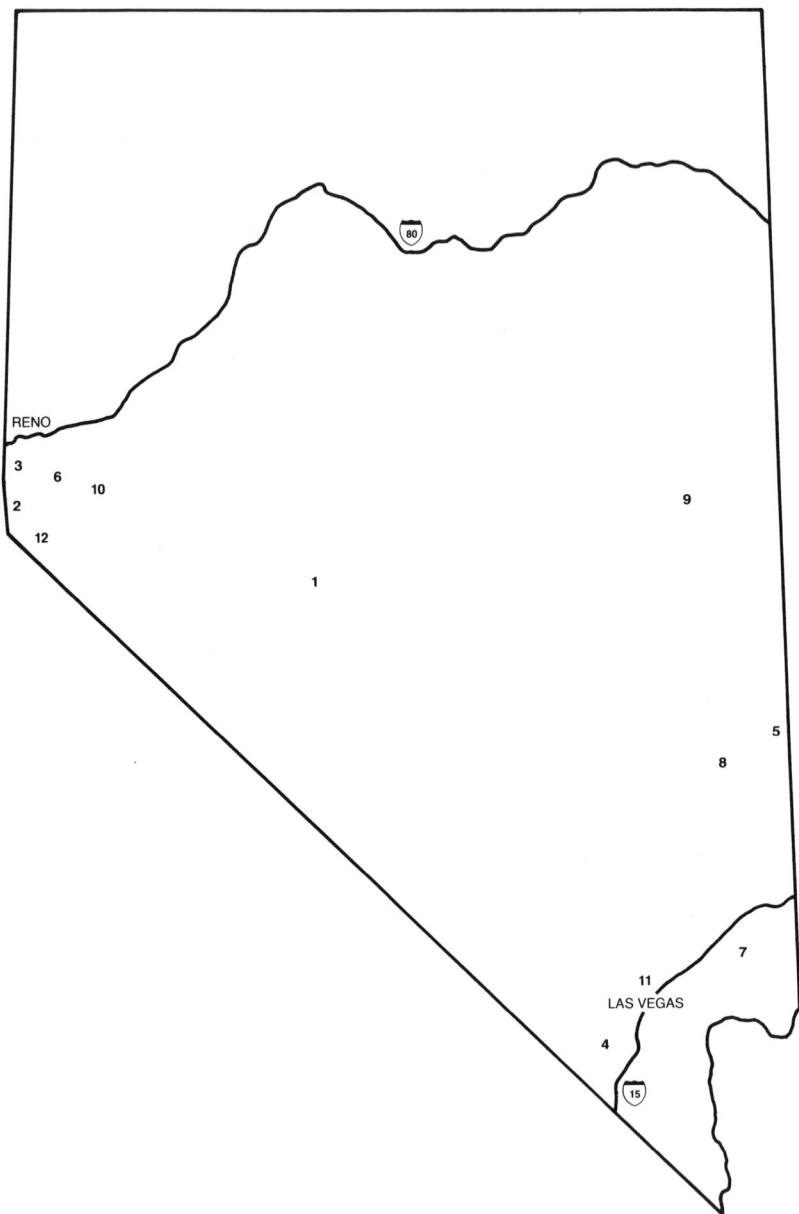

RENO

3
6
10
9
2
12
1
5
8
7
11
LAS VEGAS
4
80
15

Route 1, Box 32
Austin, Nevada 89310
No phone

LAKE TAHOE NEVADA STATE PARK
2

LOCATION - The park is located on the eastern shore of Lake Tahoe on Nevada 28.

FEATURES - Lake Tahoe is the largest alpine lake and the second deepest in North America. Only Crater Lake in Oregon is deeper. The lake has 71.5 miles of shoreline with 42.5 miles in California and 29 in Nevada.

ACTIVITIES - The park is for day use only with the exception of two backpacking campgrounds.

With its three-mile shoreline, Sand Harbor Beach, located four miles south of Incline Village off Nevada 28, has one of the best swimming beaches on the lake. Lifeguards are on duty from Memorial Day through Labor Day. Water temperatures average 68 degrees during the summer.

You can also go boating from the ramp or scuba dive in the special cove. Most divers wear wetsuits because of the cold water. Be sure to arrive at this beach early. When the parking lot's full, it's closed.

Trails from here go to Cave Rock, Memorial Point, Hidden Beach and to Spooner Lake in the Marlette/Hobart backcountry. You can also go boating, sailing, windsurfing, fishing, horseback riding in the backcountry, enjoy a picnic and camp in the campground.

At Sand Harbor, you can attend Shakespeare plays presented in August or the Lake Tahoe Music Festival presented in July.

At Cave Rock, you can enjoy shore fishing, boating from the ramp, driving 10 miles to Spooner Lake for a picnic or taking a couple of hikes. One trail goes 1.5-miles around the lake, while another goes five miles to Marlette Lake.

Hidden Beach, 1.5-miles north of Sand Harbor off Nevada 28, is a popular site for swimming and sunbathing. Hikes from here range in length from 1.6-miles around the lake to 16-miles one way if you hike from Hidden Beach to Spooner Lake. Park either at Memorial Point or at Sand Harbor.

Ride aboard the M.S. Dixie which is moored in the Zephyr Cove Marina: 702-588-3508. The Tahoe Queen is moored at the Ski Run Marina on Ski Run Boulevard off U.S. 50 in South Lake Tahoe: 916-541-4652. The end of May, you can watch the Great Lake Tahoe Sternwheeler race between these two boats. For information: 916-541-3364.

In June, watch the Super Run at South Lake Tahoe. Two amateur runners from each of the states compete for a million dollars in prize money in a 10K-foot race. Information: 702-544-5050.

In August, the Coors International Classic Bicycle Racers hold one of their stages here. Also in August, you can attend the antique boat show in North and South Tahoe.

Triathletes might want to test their skills in the "World's Toughest Triathlon" held in September at South Lake Tahoe.

Watch the Lake Tahoe calendar for a presentation by the Washoe Indians who make Tahoe their summer home. They give crafts demonstrations and perform traditional dances.

Nearby airports include Carson, Douglas County, Lake Tahoe and Reno International.

INFORMATION -
Lake Tahoe Nevada State Park
P.O. Box 3283
Incline Village, Nevada 89418
702-831-0494

WASHOE LAKE STATE PARK
3

LOCATION - Between Reno and Carson City on U.S. 395.

FEATURES - At one time the lake covered the whole valley floor, but has shrunk to its current size of four miles by two miles.

ACTIVITIES - Picnic or camp in one of 25 spots, where drinking water is available. A boat landing makes fishing, sailing and windsurfing possible. You can also go hunting or take a horseback ride in the dunes.

A steep hike from the Davis Creek Group Use Area goes to Price Lake past Slide Mountain and Rock Lake.

INFORMATION -
Washoe Lake State Park
4855 East Lake Boulevard
Carson City, Nevada 89701
702-885-4319

SPRING MOUNTAIN RANCH STATE PARK
4

LOCATION - Fifteen miles west of Las Vegas via West Charleston Boulevard, Nevada 159.

ACTIVITIES - The park is located on the Old Spanish Trail. The main ranch house is open as a visitor center Saturday, Sunday and holidays. Guided tours are offered. You can take a self-guided tour of the grounds any time.

Contact the park for information on the Super Summer Production held June through August.

A strenuous 2.5-mile hike up Sandstone Canyon requires some bouldering and can be ranger-led, if your timing is right. Camping is also available in the park.

INFORMATION -
Spring Mountain Ranch State Park
Box 124
Blue Diamond, Nevada 89004
702-875-4141

SPRING VALLEY STATE PARK
5

LOCATION - Eighteen-miles east of Pioche via Nevada 322.

FEATURES - Pioche was one of the wildest mining camps in the west as evidenced by "Boot Row" where 75 men who died violently are buried.

ACTIVITIES - The 65-acre reservoir is open year round and offers hiking, fishing, boating from the ramp and camping in one of 37 sites with drinking water. Camping is generally done from mid-April through mid-November, but the campground is open year-round.

If you stay in Pioche, you can attend Burro Days, a three-day spring celebration held over Father's Day weekend. It includes a fishing derby and burro races at Eagle Valley Reservoir.

Heritage Days with historic vignettes is presented at the Million Dollar Courthouse in July. In September, you can attend the Pioche Labor Day celebration.

For information on any of these and other festivities, call 702-962-5205.

INFORMATION -
Spring Valley State Park
Star Route 89063

Pioche, Nevada 89043
702-962-5102

DAYTON STATE PARK
6

LOCATION - Twelve miles east of Carson City on U.S. 50 on the Carson River.

FEATURES - The park was once used as a Washoe Indian campground. Both gold and silver have been mined here. By 1861, the first ore crushing stamp mill was built in Dayton and continued to operate until the 1920s when silver mining declined. The mill is still visible.

ACTIVITIES - Go boating, fishing or camp in one of 10 sites where drinking water is available. You can also hike the nature trail.

INFORMATION -
Dayton State Park
P.O. Box 412
Dayton, Nevada 89403
702-885-5678

VALLEY OF FIRE STATE PARK
7

LOCATION - Take I-15 northeast of Las Vegas for 55 miles. Turn right on Nevada 169 to continue into the park. It's 60 miles north via the Lake Mead North Shore Road. Since the park has no service stations, be sure to leave Las Vegas with a full tank of gas.

FEATURES - The park's colorful rock formations were formed 150 million years ago by the shifting of large sand dunes which gradually hardened into sandstone formations of spirals, domes and beehives. There is evidence that the area was inhabited by the Basketmakers and later by the Anasazi Pueblo farmers from 300 B.C. to 1150 A.D. You can see examples of their pictographs at Atlatl Rock.

The area experiences mild winters, but summer-time temperatures are often over 100 degrees and sometimes reach 120 degrees. Spring and fall is the best time to visit.

ACTIVITIES - Tour the visitor center, open daily from 8:30 until 4:30. You can camp in one of two campgrounds with 50 units, located at the west end of the park. Picnic areas are located at Atlatl Rock, Seven Sisters, the Cabins and near Mouse's Tank trailhead.

Hiking possibilities include a seven-mile backcountry hike to White Domes. Check to see if you can get on one that is led by the rangers by calling 702-397-2080. A five-mile hike goes to Desert Wash, while a shorter half-mile hike may be made to Mouse's Tank. A three-mile hike leaves the Rainbow Vista parking area for Fire Canyon/Silica Dome.

Drive by to see the petrified wood logs that were washed into the area 225 million years ago.

Lake Mead National Recreation Area is close by and is one of the largest man-made bodies of water in the world. Overton Beach is closest to the Valley of Fire, where you can get gas, food and lodging at the Robbins Nest Mobile Village: 702-397-2364.

INFORMATION -
Valley of Fire State Park
P.O. Box 515
Overton, Nevada 89040
702-385-026

CATHEDRAL GORGE STATE PARK
8

LOCATION - Five miles northeast of Panaca via U.S. 93.

FEATURES - The area was covered by a freshwater lake where many sediments were laid down. Gradually, the lake drained and erosion began taking its toll on the sediments of clay and siltstone creating canyons and gullies. The "caves" area on the east side of the gorge aren't true caves, but the canyon walls were so narrow that early visitors felt as though they were inside caves.

Panaca was once billed as "the toughest town in the west."

Temperatures in the winter can go below freezing and soar above 100 degrees during the summer.

ACTIVITIES - Tour the "million dollar" court house.

Camp where 116 sites await you, along with showers, drinking water and shaded picnic facilities. Hike along the trails to get a closer view of the geological features.

INFORMATION -
Cathedral Gorge State Park
Panaca, Nevada 89402
702-728-4467

CAVE LAKE STATE RECREATION AREA AND WARD CHARCOAL OVENS

9

LOCATION - Eight miles south of Ely via U.S. 93, then seven miles east on Success Summit Road.

FEATURES - There are six 30-foot high beehive-shaped charcoal ovens built in 1876 to provide fuel for the nearby smelters. The lake offers a scenic mountain setting at 7,000 feet.

ACTIVITIES - Picnic, boat and enjoy year round fishing. Camp in one of 20 campsites where drinking water is provided.

INFORMATION -
Cave Lake State Recreation Area and Ward Charcoal Ovens
P.O. Box 761
Ely, Nevada 89301
702-289-4497

FORT CHURCHILL STATE HISTORICAL PARK

10

LOCATION - Eight miles south of Silver Springs via U.S. 95A, then one mile west on Nevada 2B

FEATURES - The park occupies what was once an army outpost built around 1860 for protection against Indian attacks. The officers guarded the Pony Express Routes, along with the Overland Stage Route, the only transcontinental stagecoach route operating after the closing of the southern Butterfield route.

ACTIVITIES - The fort itself is in ruins, but is gradually being restored. You can stop at the visitor center where on Saturdays and Sundays during the summer, the park rangers dress as soldiers and give talks on early life in the fort. Each Sunday in July, the rangers lead tours through the fort at 11:00 A.M.

You can also camp year-round in one of 20 sites shaded by cottonwood trees, complete with drinking water and picnicking facilities.

In May, take the annual 12-mile canoe trip to Lahontan. Bring your own canoe, life jackets and a day's provisions.

INFORMATION -
Fort Churchill State Historical Park
Silver Springs, Nevada 89429
702-577-2345

FLOYD LAMB STATE PARK
11

LOCATION - In Las Vegas at 9200 Tule Springs Road.

ACTIVITIES - Tours are offered on Sundays at 2:00 P.M. in April, May, September and October through the historic Tules Springs Ranch buildings. Check with the park rangers for actual dates and times.

INFORMATION -
Floyd Lamb State Park
702-645-1998
   or
Nevada Division of State Parks
Capitol Complex
Carson City, Nevada 89710
702-885-4384

MORMON STATION HISTORIC STATE PARK
12

LOCATION - In the town of Genoa on Nevada 57 off I-395.

ACTIVITIES - The station, Nevada's first non-Indian settlement and supply point along the California Trail, is the site of the state's oldest saloon where you can still get a cool drink and tour the museum. The old fort has also been rebuilt.

Nearby is a buffalo ranch and Walley's Hot Springs.

In September, the Candy Dance Arts and Crafts Fair is held, complete with barbecues and dancing.

ACTIVITIES - Because of the shallow water, ranging from six to fifteen feet, the area is popular for sailing and windsurfing. You can also waterski, swim, and fish for perch and catfish. It's also a great bird watching spot. The campground has 25 sites, but no hookups.

One of the trails to hike is the Dunes Trail which stretches one-third of a mile along some dunes, or you can take mile-long Deadman's Creek Trail.

INFORMATION -
Mormon Station State Historic Park
4855 E. Lake Boulevard
Carson City, Nevada 89701
702-885-4379

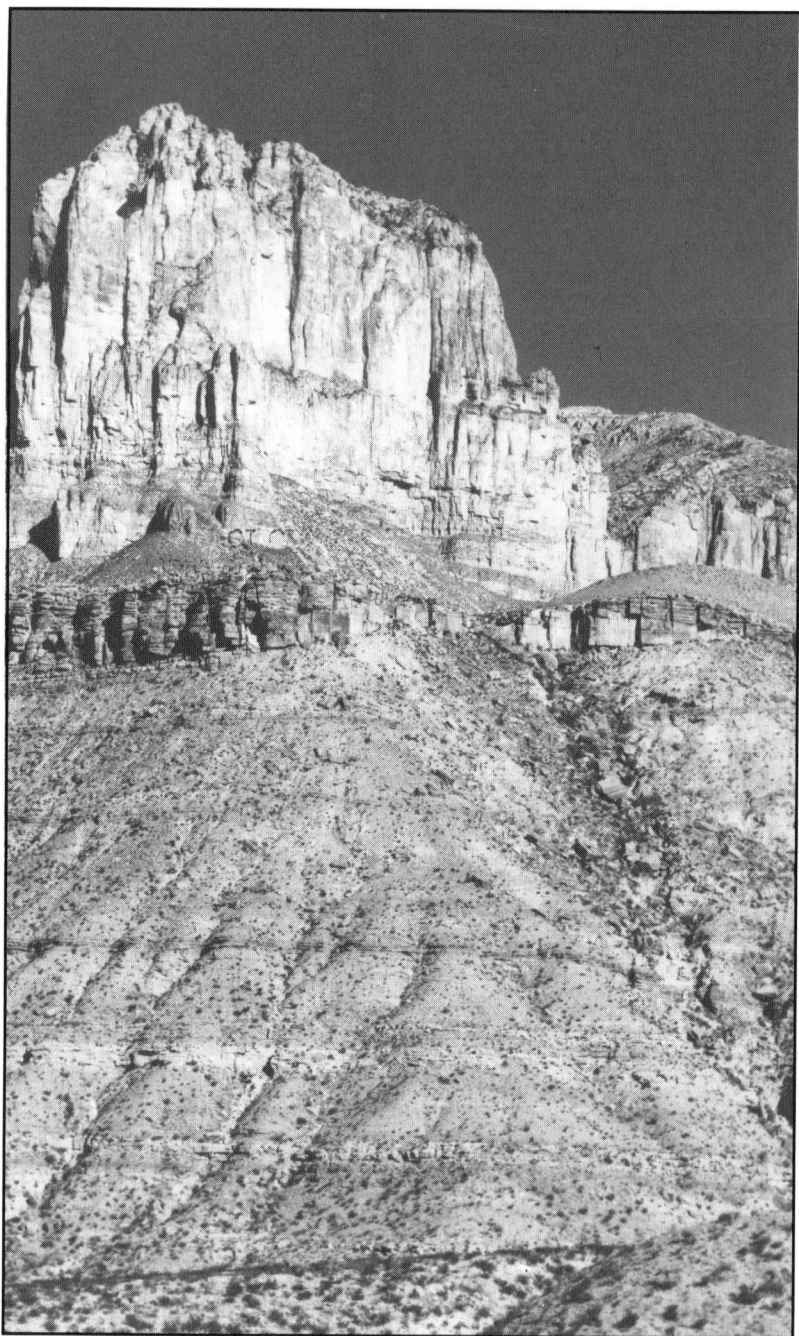

Near Living Desert State Park.
NATIONAL PARK SERVICE

NEW MEXICO

New Mexico has 45 parks which offer a wide variety of activities including whitewater sports, scuba diving, rock climbing and rock hounding. A few representative parks are included here. For a complete guide to the state's parks write: New Mexico Natural Resource Department State Park and Recreation Division P.O. Box 1147 1141 East DeVargas Street Santa Fe, New Mexico 87504-1147 505-827-7465.

BLUEWATER LAKE STATE PARK
1

LOCATION - Twenty-nine miles northwest of Grants via I-40 and New Mexico 12, and seven miles southwest of Prewitt.

ACTIVITIES - The park offers food service, facilities for camping, picnicking, hiking, boating, boat rentals, swimming and fishing. The lake is stocked with rainbow trout.

INFORMATION -
Bluewater Lake State Park
P.O. Box 3429
Prewitt, New Mexico 87045
505-876-2391

BOTTOMLESS LAKES STATE PARK
2

LOCATION - Ten miles east of Roswell via U.S. 380, then six miles south on New Mexico 409.

FEATURES - Site of the Goodnight-Loving cattle trail stop, the park has seven small lakes which are bordered by high red bluffs. They were formed

14

12

10

5

7

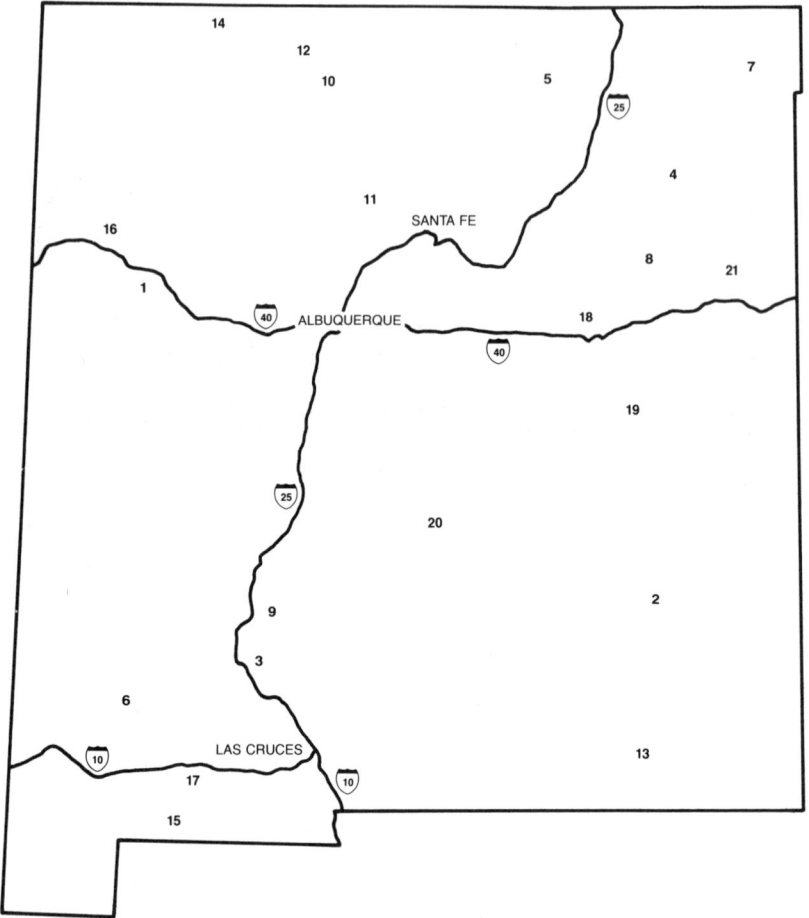

25

4

11

SANTA FE

16

8

21

1

40

ALBUQUERQUE

18

40

19

25

20

2

9

3

6

13

10

LAS CRUCES

17

10

15

as circulating water dissolved gypsum and salt deposits in the underlying rock formations. Eventually caverns were created which later collapsed because of their weight. These sinkholes filled with water which early cowboys believed were bottomless when they were unsuccessful at reaching the bottom with two of their ropes tied together. The lakes are up to 90 feet deep.

ACTIVITIES - At Lea Lake, you'll find a concession building with a cafe inside. Paddleboat rentals are available here. Swimming and scuba diving is popular because of the crystal clear waters.

You can also tour the visitor center, camp, enjoy a picnic, hike the trails, go boating where boat rentals are available, fishing, swimming and horseback riding.

A triathlon is held in early May. For information: 505-622-6250, extension 261.

INFORMATION -
Bottomless Lakes State Park
Auto Route E
Box 1200
Roswell, New Mexico 88201
505-624-6058

CABALLO LAKE STATE PARK
3

LOCATION - Fourteen miles south of Truth or Consequences on I-25.

ACTIVITIES - Fishermen can enjoy their sport year-round as they fish for bass, catfish and panfish. Visitors can also camp, picnic, swim, go boating, waterski and hike the trails. Food service and boat rentals are available.

INFORMATION -
Caballo Lake State Park
P.O. Box 32
Caballo, New Mexico 87931
505-743-3942

CHICOSA LAKE STATE PARK
4

LOCATION - Nine miles northeast of Roy and 55 miles southeast of Springer via U.S. 56, New Mexico 39 and New Mexico 120.

FEATURES - The park has historical exhibits on the early longhorn cattle drives from the Goodnight-Loving era. The trail followed by the cattlemen was 2,000 miles long and stretched from Fort Belknap on the Brazos River in northeastern Texas, to Cheyenne, Wyoming.

ACTIVITIES - Fish in the lake and camp, picnic or hike along its shores.

INFORMATION -
Chicosa Lake State Park
General Delivery
Roy, New Mexico 87743
505-485-2424

CIMARRON CANYON STATE PARK
5

LOCATION - Eight miles east of Eagle Nest on U.S. 64.

FEATURES - Four-hundred-foot high crenellated granite formations known as the Palisades.

ACTIVITIES - Enjoy excellent trout fishing along the Cimarron River, camp, go hiking in the backcountry of high mountains and deep canyons, or go rock climbing in the Palisades.

INFORMATION -
Cimarron Canyon State Park
P.O. Box 147
Ute Park, New Mexico 87749
505-377-6271

CITY OF ROCKS STATE PARK
6

LOCATION - Twenty-seven miles northwest of Deming via U.S. 180, and then three more miles northeast on New Mexico 61.

FEATURES - The tuff rock, laid down by volcanic eruptions over 33 million years ago, has been sculpted into rows of gigantic monoliths which resemble the narrow streets of a medieval village.

ACTIVITIES - You can tour the small desert botanical garden featuring plants of the southwest, camp, picnic or go hiking among the rocks.

The park is free to visitors Monday through Friday, but admission is charged on Saturday, Sunday and on holidays.

INFORMATION -
City of Rocks State Park

P.O. Box 50
Faywood, New Mexico 88034
505-536-2800

CLAYTON LAKE STATE PARK
7

LOCATION - Fifteen miles northwest of Clayton via New Mexico 370.

ACTIVITIES - Although the area was once filled with huge herds of buffalo, now the lake is inhabited by fishermen seeking rainbow trout, channel catfish and bass.

The park also has a campground, a courtesy dock for limited boating and a short trail to an interpretive pavillion, which overlooks around 500 tracks left behind by dinosaurs that roamed the area approximately 100 million years ago.

INFORMATION -
Clayton Lake State Park
Star Route
Seneca, New Mexico 88437
505-347-8808

CONCHAS LAKE STATE PARK
8

LOCATION - Thirty-four miles east of Las Vegas via New Mexico 104.

ACTIVITIES - The lake is 25 miles long and provides two marinas, boating, waterskiing, swimming and fishing for walleye and crappie.

The best developed of the park's two recreational sites is on the south side of the lake. It offers camping and picnicking, a nine-hole golf course, a 4,800-foot paved airstrip, lodge with restaurant and a general store. The northern shore has rental cabins, trailer park, restaurant, general store, marina and community bathhouse.

INFORMATION -
Conchas Lake State Park
P.O. Box 976
Conchas Dam, New Mexico 88416
505-868-2270

ELEPHANT BUTTE LAKE STATE PARK
9

LOCATION - The lake is the largest and most popular one in the state and stretches north for 45 miles from Truth or Consequences. Take New Mexico 51 east for five miles to reach the lake.

ACTIVITIES - Enjoy great bass fishing which leads to many fishing tournaments. The lake is also popular for boating, water skiing, scuba diving and sailing. You can rent boats from the marinas. Scuba divers go down to see the ruins of old Fort McRae and the remains of the original site used by the Army Corps of Engineers as they were building the dam in 1912. Some divers even go spearfishing for carp and buffalo fish.

A restaurant is located at the southern end of the lake, with cabins facing the rock formation that gives the lake its name.

Tour the visitor center to learn about the cultural and natural history of the region. When the lake was originally impounded in 1916, it was the largest body of impounded water in the world.

INFORMATION -
Elephant Butte Lake State Park
P.O. Box 13
Elephant Butte, New Mexico 87935
505-744-5421

EL VADO LAKE STATE PARK
10

LOCATION - Four miles northeast of El Vado on New Mexico 112, and 27 miles southwest of Chama via New Mexico 17, U.S. 64/84 and New Mexico 112.

ACTIVITIES - The park has a boat ramp and marina for boating, waterskiing and fishing, plus excellent hiking along the 5.5-mile trail that connects El Vado and Heron Lakes. You can also camp, have a picnic, or land your small airplane on their 5,000-foot grass strip.

In February, in Chama, come for the winter carnival with cross country races along the Cumbres and Toltec Scenic Railroad. During the summer, take a very picturesque train ride aboard the narrow gauge train through the southern Rockies. Information: 505-756-2151. In August, come for Chama Days and its race, parade, rodeo and chili cook-off.

INFORMATION -
El Vado Lake State Park
P.O. Box 29

Tierra Amarilla, New Mexico 97575
No phone / Contact them via mobile radio

FENTON LAKE STATE PARK
11

LOCATION - Thirty-eight miles west of Los Alamos via New Mexico 4 and New Mexico 126.

ACTIVITIES - This park is surrounded by the Jemez Mountains and has both lake and stream fishing for rainbow trout. You can also camp, picnic, hike the five-mile trail or go boating from the boat ramp. Sail-powered or motor boats are not permitted on the lake.

In Los Alamos, tour Bradbury Science Hall on Diamond Drive, one-quarter mile south of the Los Alamos Canyon Bridge, to see artifacts of the atomic bomb plus exhibits on modern weapons research. Free programs are presented Tuesday-Friday 9-5, and Saturday through Monday from 1-5. Information: 505-667-4444

INFORMATION -
Fenton Lake State Park
P.O. Box 555
Jemez Springs, New Mexico 87025
505-829-3630

HERON LAKE STATE PARK
12

LOCATION - Twenty-three miles southwest of Chama via New Mexico 17, U.S. 64/84 and New Mexico 95.

ACTIVITIES - The lake has excellent sailing. Motorboats can only operate at trolling speed. Fishermen can try their luck at catching trout and salmon. The park also has camping, picnicking sites and boat ramps.

Hike the 5.5-mile trail that connects El Vado with Heron Lake.

INFORMATION -
Heron Lake State Park
P.O. Box 31
Rutheron, New Mexico 87563
505-588-7470

LIVING DESERT STATE PARK
13

LOCATION - Four miles northwest of Carlsbad on U.S. 285 in the Ocotillo Hills.

ACTIVITIES - The park is open for day use only, and admission is charged.

The park has displays of the Chihuahuan Desert zone, one of four deserts on the North American continent. It's on top of a mesa where you can see over 50 species of animals, birds, prairie dogs and reptiles living in their native habitats. It has both an indoor and outdoor museum with over 1,000 varieties of Chihuahuan deserts plants along a 1.5-mile trail, and more than 1,000 varieties of cacti and succulents in a greenhouse.

Hike through the sand dunes, desert uplands and arroyo area where javelinas live. See the underground exhibit featuring nocturnal animals.

INFORMATION -
Living Desert State Park
P.O. Box 100
Carlsbad, New Mexico 88220
505-887-5516

NAVAJO LAKE STATE PARK
14

LOCATION - Twenty-four miles east of Aztec via New Mexico 173 and New Mexico 511 or 23 miles northeast of Bloomington on New Mexico 511.

ACTIVITIES - The park has three recreation areas: Pine, Sims Mesa and San Juan River. It overlooks the largest lake in northwestern New Mexico. The west side of the lake at Pine River is the most highly developed. It has camping, picnicking, a boat ramp, visitor center and good fishing for trout, salmon, bass, catfish and crappie. A concession stand has boat rentals and supplies.

The east side of the lake at Sims Mesa has camping, a boat ramp and a marina.

The San Juan River Recreation Area below the dam boasts excellent trout fishing, complete with elevated fishing platforms. You can also hike paved trails or camp here.

Pilots can fly into the nearby 5,000-foot paved strip.

INFORMATION -
Navajo Lake State Park
Pine Recreation Area
1448 New Mexico 511 #1

Navajo Dam, New Mexico 8719
505-632-2278

PANCHO VILLA STATE PARK
15

LOCATION - South of Columbus on New Mexico 11.

FEATURES - The park is the site of Pancho Villa's raid into American territory in 1916. You can still see a few of the original buildings from Camp Furlong where General Pershing was camped before continuing 400 miles into Mexico where he and 10,000 soldiers searched for Villa for 11 months. The military expedition marked the first time that U.S. military employed mechanized vehicles, cars, trucks and planes. They often carried fuel for their vehicles on pack mules.

ACTIVITIES - Tour the visitor center and watch an award-winning film on the raid plus its aftermath. Walk through the botanical desert garden which features approximately 500 different kinds of cactus.

The campground has 61 sites with water and electricity.

INFORMATION -
Pancho Villa State Park
P.O. Box 224
Columbus, New Mexico 88029
505-531-2711

RED ROCKS STATE PARK
16

LOCATION - Eight miles east of Gallup on I-40 and New Mexico 566.

ACTIVITIES - Tour the Red Rock Museum which traces the southwestern Indians' culture to see some good exhibits of their arts and crafts.

Hike one of two nature trails or camp at the foot of the huge red sandstone buttes.

The first week in August in the park, an annual square dance festival is held. Information: 505-863-4809. The second week in August, attend the annual Inter-Tribal Indian Ceremonial, a four-day event which features a rodeo, tribal games and great displays of crafts.

In early April in Gallup, attend the annual square dance festival. For information: 505-863-4809.

INFORMATION -
The park has no office to contact.

ROCKHOUND STATE PARK
17

LOCATION - Take New Mexico 11 south from Deming to the turn-off to the park located on the western slope of the Little Florida Mountains.

ACTIVITIES - Many rock and mineral specimens are found in the park by rock hounders who are permitted to remove 15-20 pounds of rocks per person. You can pick up jasper, quartz crystals, chalcedony, rhyolite, geodes, agates and opals. NOTE: The mines in the area are considered to be very unsafe. You can also camp, have a picnic or go hiking.

INFORMATION -
Rockhound State Park
P.O. Box 1064
Deming, New Mexico 88030
505-546-1212

SANTA ROSA LAKE STATE PARK
18

LOCATION - Seven miles north of Santa Rosa off 8th Street on New Mexico 91.

ACTIVITIES - Hike the three-quarter-mile long nature trail. Also enjoy water sports, boating from the boat ramp, picnicking, camping, horseback riding and cruising the bike trails. The lake has year-round fishing with trout being caught in the winter, catfish and crappie in April, and bass and walleye in the summer.

Santa Rosa Days is held over the Memorial Day weekend and features a golf tournament, a 10K race, scuba exhibitions, fishing contests and a car show. Information: 505-472-3763.

In August, attend the annual Saint Rose of Lima Fiesta.

Nearby is Blue Hole, a popular spot for scuba divers. In late June, a scuba fest is held which offers diving competitions, rock hunting, a navigation course and fin races.

INFORMATION -
Santa Rosa Lake State Park
P.O. Box 384

Santa Rosa, New Mexico 88435
505-472-3110

SUMNER LAKE STATE PARK
19

LOCATION - Sixteen miles northwest of Fort Sumner via U.S. 85 and New Mexico 203.

ACTIVITIES - Enjoy water activities such as boating, water skiing and fishing for bass, crappie, channel catfish and walleye. You can also camp or have a picnic by the water.

Fort Sumner State Monument is 23 miles southeast of the lake. It was the site of a U.S. military post established in 1862 to guard Apache and Navajo prisoners on the Bosque Redondo Reservation following the 400-mile "Long Walk" made by the Navajos.

INFORMATION -
Sumner Lake State Park
Alamo Route, Box 30
Fort Sumner, New Mexico 88119
505-355-2540

VALLEY OF FIRES STATE PARK
20

LOCATION - Three miles northwest of Carrizozo on U.S. 380.

FEATURES - The park is located on a lava flow believed to be one of the youngest in the U.S. It originated at Little Black Peak between 1,500 and 2,000 years ago. The flow covered an area of around 44 miles and is up to 70 feet deep. Named from an Indian account of the old volcanic eruption which created a "valley of fires," it's one of the best preserved lava fields in the U.S.

ACTIVITIES - Follow the self-guided nature trail through the twisted lava. Camp or picnic.

A nearby attraction is Smokey Bear Historical State Park in Capitan, 20 miles east of Carrizozo. It was established to honor the bear cub rescued from a forest fire to become the most famous bear in the United States.

INFORMATION -
Valley of Fires State Park
P.O. Box 871

Carrizozo, New Mexico 88301
No phone available

UTE LAKE STATE PARK
21

LOCATION - Twenty-seven miles northeast of Tucumcari via U.S. 54 and New Mexico 504 or two miles southwest of Logan on New Mexico 18.

ACTIVITIES - Fish for both white and largemouth bass, crappie and channel catfish. Camp or have a picnic, take a hike or go boating from the ramp where rentals are available. A lodge and cabins are located on the lake.

INFORMATION -
Ute Lake State Park
P.O. Box 52
Logan, New Mexico 88426
505-487-2284

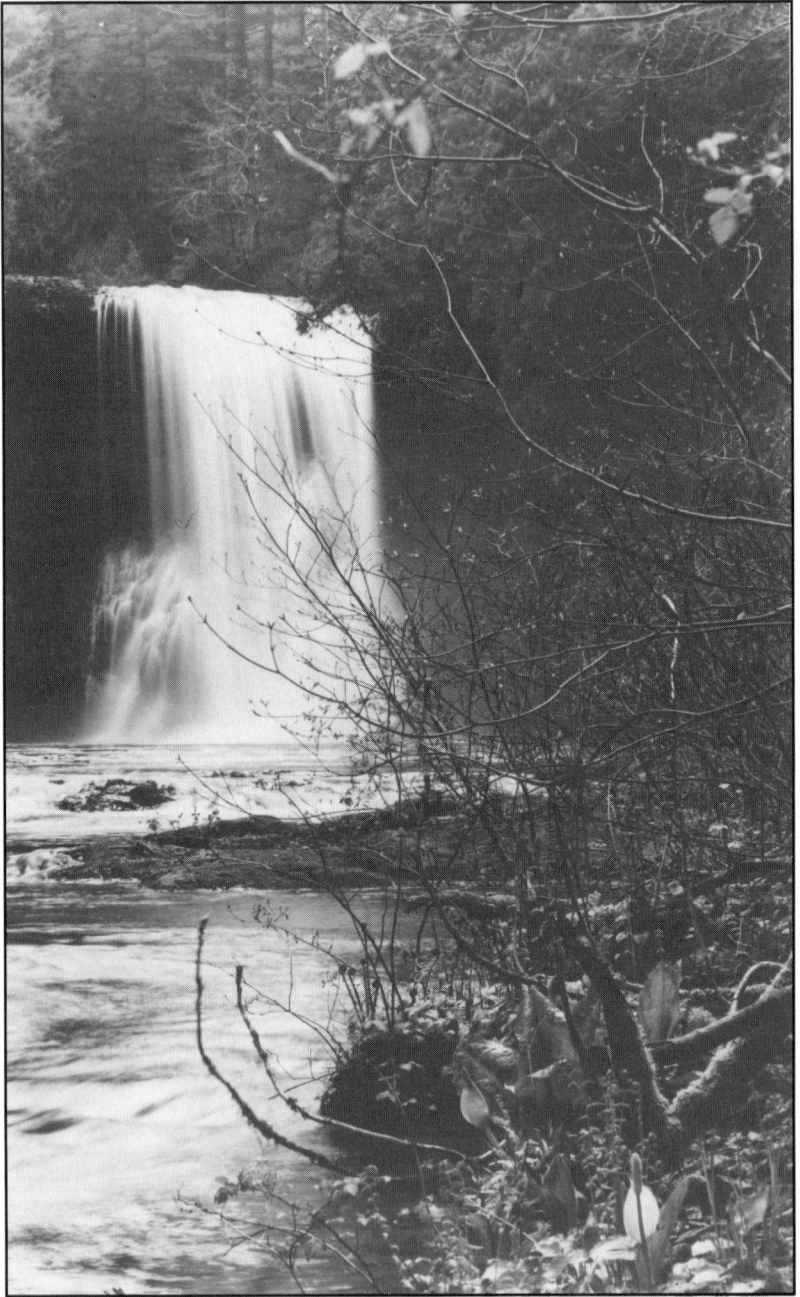

Upper North Falls, one of the 14 waterfalls within the confines of Oregon's Silver Falls State Park.

OREGON

Campground reservations are accepted in 13 of the parks from Memorial Day through Labor Day. No telephone reservations are accepted. Advance deposits are required with the reservation. For current information on campsites: 1-800-452-5687 (within Oregon) or 503-238-7488 outside of Oregon. This number may also be used for reservation cancellation. For additional information on the state parks, contact Oregon State Parks, 525 Trade Street S.E., Salem, Oregon, 97310; 503-378-6305.

All the campgrounds are open from mid-April through late October with 13 of them open year-round.

Oregon boasts over 8,000 miles of trails throughout the state, ranging from those that follow the Pacific coastline to others through the Cascades or in the High Desert in the Great Basin.

Hikers looking for a good backpacking trip can traverse the 64-mile long Oregon Coast Trail starting from Fort Stevens State Park in the north to Garibaldi in the south. You'll pass through five state parks and across numerous beaches.

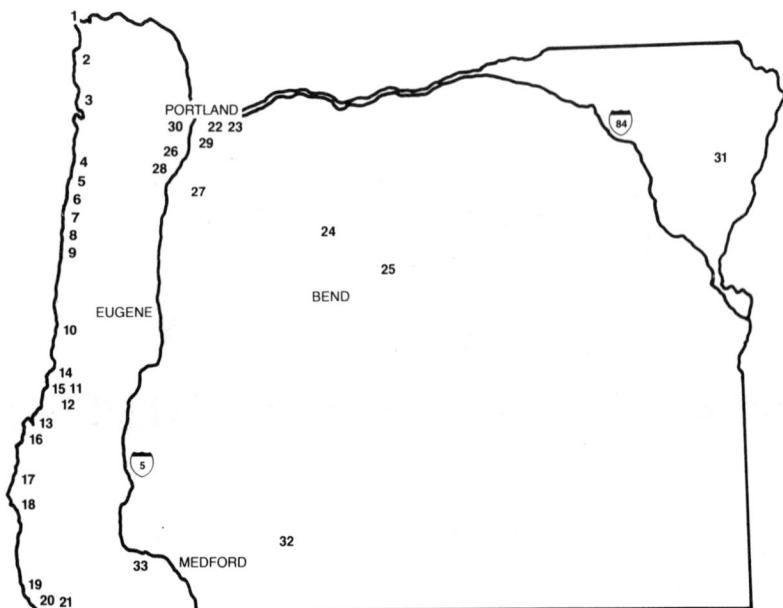

PORTLAND

30
26
28
27

22 23
29

24

25

BEND

EUGENE

10

14
15 11
12
13
16

17
18

5

32

33 MEDFORD

19
20 21

1
2
3
4
5
6
7
8
9

31

84

COASTAL PARKS ALONG U.S. 101

These parks lie along the ocean's rocky shoreline, and are good for whale watching.

FORT STEVENS STATE PARK
1

LOCATION - The park is four miles off U.S. 101, and 10 miles west of Astoria on a coastal lake near the beginning of the Columbia River.

ACTIVITIES - Fort Stevens is located on the grounds of an old military fort which protected the Columbia River's entrance beginning with the Civil War and continuing through World War II. Summertime tours are given in a vintage U.S. Army truck which takes visitors past the old buildings and fortifications.

Take a self-guided walking tour of the grounds to see some of the old gun batteries and the guardhouse. Naturalists lead tours through the Battery Mishler, constructed in 1897. Tour the interpretive center which was used earlier as a war games building but now houses artifacts from the fort's history.

Watch for the rusting hulk of the Peter Iredale, a four-masted British ship that went aground in 1906.

The park marks the beginning of the 64-mile Oregon Coast Trail. It has good picnic facilities for club camping, group tent facilities and a boat dock and ramp. You can also go clamming or hiking in the area.

INFORMATION -
Fort Stevens State Park
Hammond, Oregon 97121
503-861-1671

ECOLA STATE PARK
2

LOCATION - Two miles north of Cannon Beach off U.S. 101.

ACTIVITIES - The park is near the end of the Lewis and Clark Trail where you can see sea lion and bird rookeries on the offshore rock formations. Hike the cliff trail, picnic, fish, or go swimming. Camp in the hike-in campground in Indian Creek.

INFORMATION -
Ecola State Park
Astoria Area Chamber of Commerce
Department W
P.O. Box 176
Astoria, Oregon 97814
503-523-6311

CAPE KIWANDA, CAPE LOOKOUT AND CAPE MEARES
3

LOCATION - All three parks are west of Tillamook off U.S. 101.

ACTIVITIES - You can drive, cycle or hike a 20-mile loop along "The Three Capes Scenic Loop." The route encompasses all three parks. Follow the Scenic Drive signs from Tillamook or Pacific City.

Cape Meares is ten miles west of Tillamook. Tour the historic lighthouse erected in 1890. It's only open during the summer. Take a hike to a good lookout, or go to see Octopus Tree, a large Sitka spruce that's 50 feet tall. Cape Meares has a rain forest and sculpted sandstone cliffs. A national wildlife refuge is located offshore. Bikers and hikers can camp here.

Cape Kiwanda is one mile north of Pacific City and has a colorful sandstone headland and a spectacular ocean view. It's also a favorite for rock climbers who enjoy scaling the rocky cliffs. Watch for hang gliders soaring off the high dunes and offshore rocks. The ocean waves are usually populated with surfers.

Cape Lookout, located 12 miles southwest of Tillamook, is one of Oregon's most primitive ocean shore areas. It's located on an ancient lava flow that extends into the ocean for two miles. If you drive to the summit, you can hike 2.5-miles through a forest of hemlock and cedar to the tip of an overlook where you can get a good view of the coast. Stay alert since there are steep drop offs along the way. As you hike, watch for nesting sea birds. The park has a wide beach from which surfers and fishermen enjoy their sport. There are two self-guided nature trails, and the area is popular for clamming and enjoying the wildflowers. Three miles of the Oregon Coast Trail pass through here.

Both Cape Kiwanda and Cape Lookout are open for day use only. Cape Lookout has the only camping facilities for 152 tents, 75 sites with electrical hookups, and 52 with full hookups. They accept reservations. It also offers a

hiker/biker campground.
INFORMATION -
Cape Lookout State Park
13000 Whiskey Creek Road West
Tillamook, Oregon 97141
503-842-4981

DEVIL'S LAKE STATE PARK
4

LOCATION - The park is northwest of Lincoln City on U.S. 101.

ACTIVITIES - You can go fishing, boating, or swimming in either salt water or in fresh water. One campground has 100 sites with 32 providing full hookups. A special hiker/biker campground is located in the park. Campground reservations: 1452 N.E. 6th, Lincoln City, 97367.

A covered bridge is on Upper Drift Creek 2.5-miles south of Lincoln City. To reach it, follow U.S. 101 to Upper Drift Creek Road.

INFORMATION -
Devil's Lake State Park
1452 N.E. 6th
Lincoln City, Oregon 97367
503-994-2002

FOGARTY CREEK STATE PARK
5

LOCATION - Two miles north of Depoe Bay on U.S. 101.

ACTIVITIES - Enjoy a forested picnic area and a small walking beach from which you can fish.

INFORMATION -
Chamber of Commerce
Department W
555 S.W. Coast Highway
Newport, Oregon 97365
503-265-8801

DEVIL'S PUNCHBOWL STATE PARK
6

LOCATION - Eight miles north of Newport off U.S. 101.

FEATURES - The park was named for a hole in the sandstone terrace created when the roof of two sea caves collapsed. You can watch the incoming tides surge into the bowl. If the seas are stormy, the punchbowl resembles a boiling cauldron.

ACTIVITIES - Hike down the short trail to the Marine Gardens Ocean Shore Preserve to watch sea creatures in their natural habitats. Surfers here should wear either wet or dry suits since the water is quite cold.

INFORMATION -
Newport Chamber of Commerce
Department W
555 S.W. Coast Highway
Newport, Oregon 97365
503-265-88801

BEVERLY BEACH STATE PARK
7

LOCATION - Seven miles north of Newport on U.S. 101.

ACTIVITIES - Camping is available in 276 sites with 59 full hookups. Reservations may be made by writing Star Route North, Box 684, Newport, Oregon 97365. You can also enjoy the special hiker/biker camp, picnic, hike the one-mile trail, go saltwater fishing or beachcombing.

INFORMATION -
Beverly Beach State Park
Star Route North, Box 684
Newport, Oregon 97365
503-265-9278

YAQUINA BAY STATE PARK
8

LOCATION - The park is located on a bluff at the north end of the Yaquina Bay Bridge along U.S. 101 near Newport.

ACTIVITIES - Enjoy a picnic at one of the picnic tables nestled under twisted trees sculpted by the incessant ocean winds. Tour the Yaquina Bay

Lighthouse built in 1871 and now used as a museum. It's closed from October-April, and then is open on Friday, Saturday and Sunday from 12-4. It's furnished with authentic pieces representative of the 1870s. The lighthouse was abandoned after only three years of use since ships were unable to see its light because of the protruding headland.

Rent a boat and fish for salmon, chinook and coho. Go clamming, but watch out for the soft mud. Crabbing is best either at high or low tide, or you can enjoy surf fishing for perch, trout, lingcod and black rockfish.

Go windsurfing or sailing. A local sailing club sponsors a couple of regattas each year.

Fly a kite at the Red, White and Blue Kite Festival held in mid-June. Another festival is held in the fall.

In Newport, attend the Blessing of the Fleet in March; the Loyalty Days and Sea Fair Festival is held the first weekend in May; on Memorial Day, the Fleet of Flowers is held in Depoe Bay; and the Columbus Day Regatta is held in Yaquina Bay.

Visit the Undersea Gardens in the Old Bay Front district where you can watch scuba divers swimming among some of the 5,000 marine specimens.

The Chitwood covered bridge is 18 miles east of Newport on Oregon 20.

INFORMATION -
Yaquina Bay State Park
% Newport Chamber of Commerce
Department W
555 S.W. Coast Highway
Newport, Oregon 97365
503-265-8801

SOUTH BEACH STATE PARK
9

LOCATION - Two miles south of Newport on U.S. 101.

ACTIVITIES - The park has 250 sites, all with electrical hookups. For camping reservations: P.O. Box 1350, Newport, Oregon 97365. Also enjoy picnicking, hiking, swimming, saltwater fishing, camping in the hiker/biker campground and strolling along the sandy beach.

INFORMATION -
South Beach State Park
P.O. Box 1250
Newport, Oregon 97365
503-867-4715

JESSIE M. HONEYMAN STATE PARK
10

LOCATION - Three miles south of Florence on U.S. 101.

FEATURES - The park is known for its sand dunes, some 300 feet high. The park also has several lakes and wild rhododendrons which bloom profusely during the late spring and early summer.

ACTIVITIES - The park offers over 300 campsites, with 66 having full hookups. For campground reservations: 84505 Highway 101, Florence, Oregon 97439. The park has a special hiker/biker campground as well. You can also have a picnic, go hiking, fishing from the dock, boating, sailing or swimming.

Woahink Lake is not only popular for fishing and sailing, but also for its windsurfing.

Tour Sea Lion Caves, 12 miles north of Florence. Take the elevator 1,500 feet down into one of the largest sea caves in the world to watch sea lions, birds, and an occasional giant gray whale. Information: 503-547-3111.

INFORMATION -
Jessie M. Honeyman State Park
84505 Highway 101
Florence, Oregon 97439
503-997-3641

SHORE ACRES STATE PARK
11

LOCATION - Three and one-half miles south of Charleston on Cape Arago Highway, or 13 miles southwest of Coos Bay off U.S. 101.

ACTIVITIES - Flower lovers will enjoy touring this old estate which features unusual botanical gardens, and a garden house which is available for special occasions. It's open summers.

It also features spectacular ocean views with picnicking and hiking opportunities. A portion of the Oregon Coast Trail passes through the park. Watch storms moving through the area while standing in a glass-walled shelter.

INFORMATION -
Shore Acres State Park
Bay Area Chamber of Commerce
Department W
P.O. Box 210
Coos Bay, Oregon 97420
503-269-0215

GOLDEN AND SILVER STATE PARK
12

LOCATION - Twenty-four miles northeast of Coos Bay in the Coastal Range off U.S. 101.

ACTIVITIES - The park has two waterfalls, each dropping over 100 feet. You can fish, picnic or hike 1.4 miles in a forest with myrtlewood trees.

INFORMATION -
Golden and Silver State Park
Bay Area Chamber of Commerce
Department W
P.O. Box 210
Coos Bay, Oregon 97420
503-269-0215

SUNSET BAY STATE PARK
13

LOCATION - Twelve miles southwest of Coos Bay off U.S. 101.

ACTIVITIES - The campground has 22 full hookup sites and 42 for tents. For camping reservations: 13030 Cape Arago Highway, Coos Bay, Oregon 97420. You can also picnic, hike the 1.3-mile long trail, explore the sand dunes, enjoy the sandy beach, go boating, get good pictures of the inactive Cape Arago lighthouse, and go fishing.

INFORMATION -
Sunset Bay State Park
13030 Cape Arago Highway
Coos Bay, Oregon 97420
503-888-4902

UMPQUA LIGHTHOUSE STATE PARK
14

LOCATION - Five miles south of Reedsport off U.S. 101.

FEATURES - The park has 2.5-miles of shoreline and 500-foot-high sand dunes. These dunes stretch for 40 miles between North Bend and Florence. They're next to the Oregon Dunes National Recreation Area.

Unfortunately, the lighthouse here is not open to the public.

ACTIVITIES - Go camping in the campground with 22 full hookups, explore the sand dunes, get photographs of the lighthouse, picnic, hike the 1.3-mile long trail, boat, fish, swim or enjoy a horseback ride.

INFORMATION -
Umpqua Lighthouse State Park
Lower Umpqua Chamber of Commerce
Department W
P.O. Box 11-B
Reedsport, Oregon 97467
503-271-3495

WILLIAM M. TUGMAN STATE PARK
15

LOCATION - Eight miles south of Reedsport on Highway 101.

ACTIVITIES - Camp in the campground where showers and 115 electrical hookups are available, picnic, boat from the dock or ramp, fish, swim or take advantage of the special hiker/biker campground.

INFORMATION -
William M. Tugman State Park
Lower Umpqua Chamber of Commerce
Department W
P.O. Box 11-B
Reedsport, Oregon 97467
503-271-3495

BULLARD'S BEACH STATE PARK
16

LOCATION - Two miles north of Bandon on U.S. 101.

ACTIVITIES - Camp in the campground with 92 full hookups, picnic, see the exhibits, enjoy an ocean beach, horseback ride on the 3.5-mile equestrian trail, camp in the horse camp, go boating or fishing. The area has a hiker/biker campground with showers.

The lighthouse was built in 1896 and is open during the summer.

If you come to Bandon in the fall, attend their cranberry harvest. This area is one of the few places in the world where they'll grow.

INFORMATION -
Bullard's Beach State Park
503-347-2209

or
Gold Beach Chamber of Commerce
Department W.
510 South Ellensburg Avenue
Gold Beach, Oregon 97444
503-247-7526

CAPE BLANCO STATE PARK
17

LOCATION - Eleven miles northwest of Port Orford and six miles off U.S. 101.

FEATURES - The area is known for its chalky rocks, many with embedded fossil shells. The lighthouse, constructed in 1870, is still in use.

ACTIVITIES - Watch for sea lions on the offshore rocks. Tour the Hughes House built in 1898 and see its antique and antiques. It's open Wednesday-Saturday from 10-5, and on Sunday from 1-5 from mid-April through September 30. For information: 503-332-2975.

You can also camp in their campground with 58 electrical hookups, stay in the hiker/biker campground, hike the half-mile trail, or stay in the horse camp and ride the 3.5-mile equestrian trail.

INFORMATION -
Cape Blanco State Park
503-332-6774
    or
Gold Beach Chamber of Commerce
Department W
510 South Ellensburg Avenue
Gold Beach, Oregon 97444
503-247-7526

HUMBUG MOUNTAIN STATE PARK
18

LOCATION - Six miles south of Port Orford on U.S. 101. The park is nestled in the foothills of the coastal mountains a mile from the ocean.

ACTIVITIES - Picnic or camp in the mountain canyon with 30 full hookups or in the hiker/biker campground, have a picnic, go fishing, hike along the ocean beach or ascend three-miles to reach the mountain summit. The vertical cliffs of the mountain prevent the ocean waves from breaking since there is no shelf of land for them to roll on. As you hike, watch the waves sloshing up and down along the cliff face.

Part of the Oregon Coast Trail passes through here.

INFORMATION -
Humbug Mountain State Park
503-332-6774
   or
Gold Beach Chamber of Commerce
Department W.
510 So. Ellensburg Avenue
Gold Beach, Oregon 97444
503-247-7526

SAMUEL H. BOARDMAN STATE PARK
19

LOCATION - Four miles north of Brookings on U.S. 101.

FEATURES - This is one of a series of parks which stretch 11 miles along the coast. The Ocean Coast Trail passes through here.

ACTIVITIES - A special hiker/biker camp is here, along with a boat dock and ramp, spectacular ocean views, and good clam digging. Check locally for conditions.

At Lone Ranch, you can enjoy surfing, rock fishing and clamming. At Cape Ferrulo and House Rock Point, you can hike trails to the ocean. At Natural Bridge Cove, hike 50 yards to see the natural arch.

INFORMATION -
Samuel H. Boardman State Park
Brookings-Harbor Chamber of Commerce
Department W
P.O. Box 940
Brookings, Oregon 97415
503-469-3181

HARRIS BEACH
20

LOCATION - Two miles north of Brookings off U.S. 101.

FEATURES - Brookings was actually bombed on September 9, 1942, by a

Japanese plane that dropped incendiary bombs on Mount Emily, east of town. The plane had been assembled aboard a submarine off the coast, and the attack was intended to start a forest fire, but failed. After the war, the Japanese pilot returned to donate a samurai sword to the community. It's on display in Brookings City Hall.

ACTIVITIES - Camp in the campground with 34 full hookups, 51 electrical hookups and 66 tent sites. For reservations, write to the park authorities, 1655 Highway 101, Brookings, Oregon 97415. There's a special campground for hikers and bikers.

The park features an 11-mile footpath which is one of the most spectacular on the Oregon coast. It follows high cliffs, but has no railing, so use caution.

Go fishing for steelhead and salmon, clamming in the sand, swimming, boating, or take a ride on the Rogue River. Contact the Gold Beach Chamber of Commerce for information: 503-247-7526.

INFORMATION -
Harris Beach State Park
1655 Highway 101
Brookings, Oregon 97415
503-469-2021

AZALEA STATE PARK
21

LOCATION - North of Brookings and close to Harris Beach State Park off U.S. 101.

FEATURES - Some of the azalias growing here are over 300 years old and are 20 feet tall.

INFORMATION -
Azalea State Park
Brookings-Harbor Chamber of Commerce
Department W
P.O. Box 940
Brookings, Oregon 97415
503-469-3181

COLUMBIA GORGE AREA

The Columbia Gorge state parks, located in the northern part of the state, include a string of parks which lie along the edge of the Columbia River Scenic Highway and Preserve and offer both historic and geological features. Here you can see 30 million years of geological history along the gorge walls composed of old lava flows which were eroded and then later uplifted to form the Cascade Range.

The 24-mile Columbia River Highway is now designated U.S. 30. This scenic route begins near Sandy River at Troutdale and goes five miles west of Bonneville Dam. The highway is quite narrow, however, and with high traffic volume, parking may be difficult during the summer.

GUY W. TALBOT STATE PARK
22

LOCATION - Four miles west of Bridal Veil off I-84 and 27 miles east of Portland on Columbia Scenic Highway, U.S. 30.

FEATURES - The park contains the Latourell Falls, the second highest waterfall in the Columbia Gorge, dropping 249-feet. Other falls are located at Bridal Veil and Shepperd's Dell State Parks. All three parks are open for day use only.

ACTIVITIES - Hike the 3.4-mile trail to see the falls. If you visit Bridal Veil State Park, you can take the one-mile trail to see the falls. Shepperd's Dell has a short trail to the falls.

INFORMATION -
Guy W. Talbot State Park
Hood River County Chamber of Commerce
Department W
Port Marina Park
Hood River, Oregon 97031
503-386-2000

JOHN B. YEON STATE PARK
23

LOCATION - Two and one-half miles west of Bonneville off I-84, and 40 miles east of Portland on U.S. 30 Scenic Highway.

ACTIVITIES - The park is for day use only. See the Elowah Falls from the McCord Creek Trail. Hike some of the other trails to some good overlooks of the falls.

In Bonneville, tour the fish hatchery on I-84 and U.S. 30 near the dam. Also see the Bonneville Lock and Dam. Take Exit 40 off I-84 to reach the Bradford Island Visitor Center. This center has five floors of various exhibits, a three-screen movie theater, and an underwater viewing room where you can watch migrating fish coming up the fish ladder from March through November. You can also fish and picnic here.

During the summer, a boat takes you on a two-hour river cruise starting from the visitor center three times a day. The boat stops at the Cascade Locks which were built at the turn of the century to extend the Columbia River shipping route farther inland. The visitor center also has the northwest's only sternwheeler museum and memorabilia from the early paddlewheel steamers.

INFORMATION -
Guy W. Talbot State Park
Hood River County Chamber of Commerce
Department W
Port Marina Park
Hood River, Oregon 97031
503-386-2000

CENTRAL OREGON

COVE PALISADES STATE PARK
24

LOCATION - Fifteen-miles southwest of Madras off U.S. 97 on Lake Billy Chinook.

FEATURES - Round Butte Dam is located in a cove where three canyons meet.

ACTIVITIES - Reservations for the campground may be made through the park service, Route 1, Box 60 CP, Culver, Oregon, 97734.

You can also picnic, hike, boat, fish, go swimming and waterskiing. The area offers a full service marina for boaters.

The Round Butte Dam has an observation point overlooking the hydroelectric plant. It's open Wednesday-Sunday from 10-6, from June 15 through Labor Day.

INFORMATION -
Cove Palisades State Park
Route 1, Box 60 CP
Culver, Oregon 97734
503-546-3412

PRINEVILLE RESERVOIR STATE PARK
25

LOCATION - The park is 17 miles southeast of Prineville off U.S. 26.

ACTIVITIES - The area is a favorite for rockhounders who are searching for a thunderegg, the official state rock. You can also camp in their campground with 22 full hookups, go fishing, swimming, boating, waterskiing or have a picnic. The park accepts campground reservations.

INFORMATION -
Prineville Reservoir State Park
Prineville Lake Route, Box 1050
Prineville, Oregon 97754
503-447-4363

CHAMPOEG STATE PARK
26

LOCATION - Seven miles southeast of Newberg on the Willamette River off I-5 on U.S. 99.

ACTIVITIES - Attend the "Champoeg Outdoor Drama" which depicts the area's history in an outdoor amphitheater, Friday-Sunday nights at 6:30 on the last four weekends in July. To order tickets by mail: Champoeg Historical Pageant, Box 707, Newberg, Oregon 97132, or call 503-538-1800.

Tour the visitor center to learn more about the area's history and how the state government began.

Tour the Pioneer Mother's Memorial Cabin, built in 1931 as a memorial to pioneer mothers. It's open Wednesday-Sunday from noon-5 except Christmas and New Year's. Information: 503-635-2237

In the park, you can enjoy riding along paved bike paths, go boating on the Willamette River from the boat dock, go camping in the campground with 48 electrical hookups, enjoy fishing, and hiking along ten miles of hiking/biking trails.

Visit the Robert Newell House, west of the park, to see 1860 decorations housed on the first floor, and other historic artifacts on the second floor.

Tour the 1850 Butteville Jail and a pioneer school. Both are open Wednesday-Sunday from noon-5 except Christmas and New Year's.

In Newberg, tour the Hoover-Minthorn House built in 1881. It's located on S. River and E. 2nd. It is Newberg's oldest house and is where President Hoover lived for five years while he was a child. It's open Wednesday-Sunday from 1-4.

INFORMATION -
Champoeg State Park
503-678-1251
    or
Salem Area Convention and Visitors Bureau
Department W
1313 Mill street S.E.
Salem, Oregon 97301
503-581-4325

SILVER FALLS STATE PARK
27

LOCATION - Twenty-six miles east of Salem off Oregon 22 on Oregon 214.

FEATURES - The park is Oregon's largest state park and has 14 waterfalls with five of them dropping over 100 feet.

ACTIVITIES - Picnic, bike, see the exhibits, go for a horseback ride, fishing or swimming. The campground has showers, 53 hookups, and 52 tent sites. Hikers will enjoy exploring the seven-mile trail which passes ten waterfalls in the dense forest canyons. The park also has a nature lodge with a snack bar open during the summer, a 3.7-mile bike trail, a 3-mile jogging trail, a 12-mile equestrian trail and a horse camp.

INFORMATION -
Silver Falls State Park

503-873-8681
or
Salem Area Convention and Visitors Bureau
Department W
1313 Mill Street S.E.
Salem, Oregon 97301
503-581-4325

WILLAMETTE MISSION STATE PARK
28

LOCATION - The park is on the Willamette River, eight miles north of Salem on the Wheatland Ferry Road, Oregon 99W.

ACTIVITIES - The park is the site of the Jason Lee mission built in the 1830s. You can have a picnic, go hiking on the four-mile trail or horseback riding on the two-mile equestrian trail. You can also bike the bicycle paths, go boating or fishing in the river.

INFORMATION -
Willamette Mission State Park
Salem Area Convention and Visitors Bureau
Department W
1313 Mill Street S.E.
Salem, Oregon 97301
503-581-4325

MILO McIVER STATE PARK
29

LOCATION - Five miles west of Estacada on Oregon 211 on the Clackamas River.

ACTIVITIES - Camp in the campground with showers and 45 electrical hookups, picnic, fish, go for a hike, boat ride or horseback ride on the 4.5-mile equestrian trail.

INFORMATION -
Milo McIver State Park
Greater Portland Convention and Visitors Association
Department W
26 S.W. Salmon

Portland, Oregon 97204
503-222-2223

TRYON CREEK STATE PARK
30

LOCATION - Six miles southwest of Portland off I-5 on Terwilliger Boulevard.

ACTIVITIES - The park offers a natural setting within an urban area, and is popular with Portland area joggers. Hike along the eight-mile hiking trail, ride the 3.5-mile equestrian trail, bike the three-mile bike trail and tour the nature center.

INFORMATION -
Tryon Creek State Park
503-653-3166
Greater Portland Convention and Visitors Association
Department W
26 S.W. Salmon
Portland, Oregon 97204
503-222-2223

EASTERN OREGON

WALLOWA LAKE STATE PARK
31

LOCATION - Six miles south of Joseph off Oregon 82. The park is located on the southern tip of the lake.

ACTIVITIES - Wallawa Lake was formed by a glacier at the base of the rugged mountains. The area is sometimes referred to as the "Switzerland of America."

Camp in the campground with 121 full hookups or 89 tent sites. For reservations: Route 1, Box 323, Joseph, Oregon 97846. You can also have a picnic, hike into the Eagle Cap Wilderness area, boat from the marina, fish, swim, or go on a horseback ride.

Backpackers should check out the newly developed hut-to-hut camping available near the lake.

For a chartered flight over Hells Canyon National Recreation Area, contact Joseph Air Service at the park airport.

If you're in Joseph the last weekend in July, attend the Chief Joseph Days Rodeo.

INFORMATION -
Wallowa Lake State Park
503-432-4185
Route 1, Box 323
Joseph, Oregon 97846

SOUTHERN OREGON

COLLIER STATE PARK
32

LOCATION - Thirty miles north of Klamath Falls on U.S. 97.

ACTIVITIES - Camp in the campground with 50 full hookups and 18 tent sites. Enjoy a picnic, hike the 1.5-mile trail, horseback ride from the day-use hitching area, go fishing, or see the exhibits in the open-air logging museum.

INFORMATION -
Collier State Park
503-783-2471
    or
Klamath Falls Visitors and Convention Bureau
Department W.
125 North 8th Street
Klamath Falls, Oregon 97601
503-884-5193

VALLEY OF THE ROGUE STATE PARK
33

LOCATION - Twelve miles east of Grants Pass on I-5 on the Rogue River

ACTIVITIES - Camp in the campground with 97 full hookups and 22 tent sites. Also enjoy year round picnicking, boating, and fishing.

INFORMATION -

Valley of the Rogue State Park

503-582-1118

   or

Grants Pass Visitor and Convention Bureau

P.O. Box 970

206 N.E. 7th Street

Grants Pass, Oregon 97526

503-476-7717

Dead Horse Point Vista.
MARY TULLIUS

UTAH

Many travelers are already familiar with Utah's five national parks: Arches, Bryce Canyon, Canyonlands, Capitol Reef and Zion. Not many know of its state parks which provide many excellent recreational opportunities. All of Utah's state parks accept reservations for their campsites except Utah Lake State Park.

DEAD HORSE POINT STATE PARK
1

LOCATION - It's 13 miles north of Moab via Utah 191, and then 23 miles southwest on Utah 313.

FEATURES - The park has an overlook point which is 2,000 feet above Canyonlands National Park and the Colorado River Gorge. It was named after some wild mustangs who were herded into this natural rock corral and accidentally left to die of thirst. It's one of Utah's most photographed points.

ACTIVITIES - Camp in Kayenta Campground year-round at 5,900 feet with 21 units, all with electrical hookups. Hike or drive out to Dead Horse Point from the visitor center. Watch for the remains of the old wooden corral fence erected across the narrowest section of the point.

While in the area, visit Arches National Monument and hike the various trails to get close-up views of the many arches that grace the park.

Canyonlands National Park is next to Dead Horse Point State Park, where you're treated to some great views of the canyon from various overlooks.

INFORMATION -
Dead Horse Point State Park
P.O. Box 609
Moab, Utah 84532-0609
801-259-6511

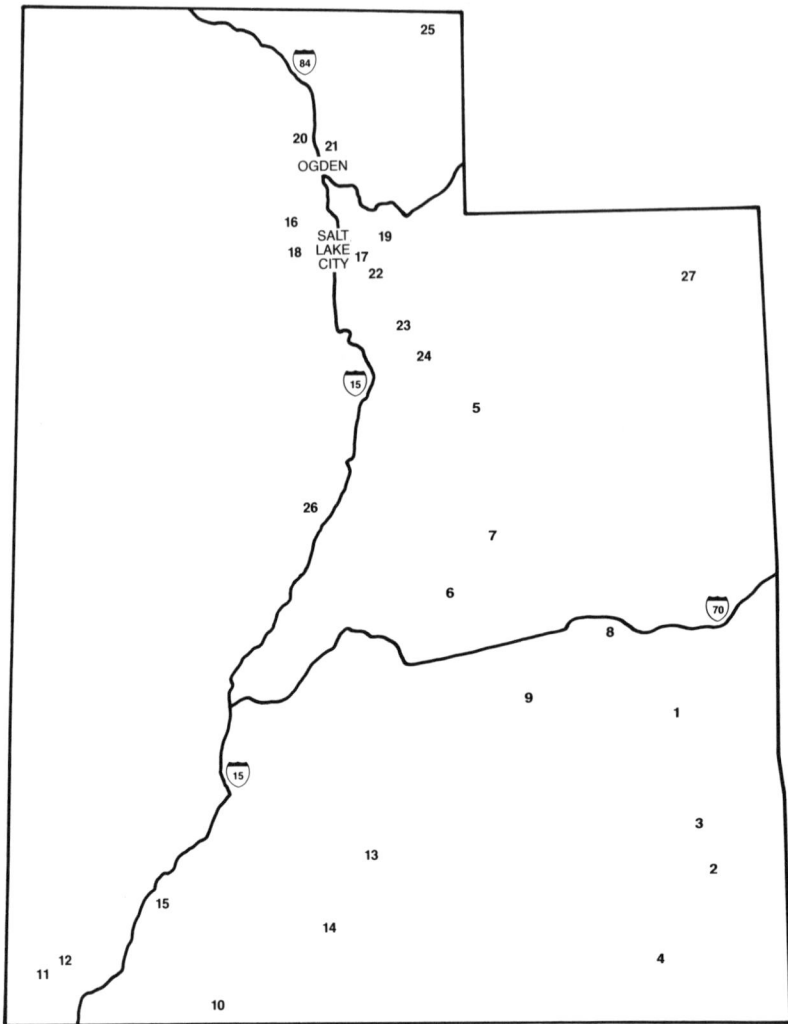

84

25

20 21
OGDEN

16
SALT
LAKE   19
18
CITY   17
22

27

23

24

5

15

26

7

6

70

8

9

1

13

3

2

15

14

4

11 12

10

EDGE OF THE CEDARS STATE PARK
2

LOCATION - The park is located off U.S. 191 at 660 West 400 North Street near Blanding in southeastern Utah.

FEATURES - The park emphasizes the structural remains of some dwellings and ceremonial complexes built by Indians who lived here between 750 and 1150 A.D.

ACTIVITIES - Tour the newly constructed museum erected on the site of an Anasazi ruin to see various artifacts of the pre-historic Anasazi, Navajo and Ute Indians plus displays on the early Anglo settlers. The museum contains one of the largest Anasazi pottery collections in the southwest.

Anyone interested in ancient Indian cultures and petroglyphs can hike or drive sections of the "Trail of the Ancients." This 100-mile trail passes through the four corners of Utah, Colorado, Arizona and New Mexico, seven national parks, 21 national monuments, numerous national forests, and two state parks: Edge of the Cedars and Goosenecks. It was designed to give the traveler a better idea about the prehistoric and modern Indian cultures, early pioneer life, as well as the effects that nature has had in shaping the land. You can enter the trail at any point. For further information and a map, contact the San Juan Travel Council, Box 490, Monticello, Utah 84535; 801-587-2231, ext. 29.

In nearby Blanding, you can also see art and photo exhibits.

To-sight see from the air, go to the Blanding Airport to take one of their flights: 801-678-3222

INFORMATION -
Edge of the Cedars State Park
P.O. Box 788
Blanding, Utah 84511
801-678-2238

NEWSPAPER ROCK STATE PARK
3

LOCATION - Fifteen miles north of Monticello, then 11 miles southwest of U.S. 163/191 on Utah 211.

FEATURES - The park is famous for its 350 Indian petroglyphs sketched on a large flat rock and dating from three distinct periods. The cliff mural is one of Utah's archaeological treasures.

ACTIVITIES - Picnic or enjoy primitive camping in the campground at

5,400 feet. It's open year-round and has 10 tent sites, but no drinking water.

INFORMATION -
Newspaper Rock State Park
% Southeast Region Office
125 West 200 North
Moab, Utah 84532-2330
801-259-8151

GOOSENECKS OF THE SAN JUAN STATE PARK
4

LOCATION - Four miles north of Mexican Hat on U.S. 163, then west on Utah 261 for four more miles.

FEATURES - The gooseneck is located in a 1,000-foot deep chasm and was named for the deep meander made by the San Juan River. Created as the land rose, the cutting ability of the river never broke the curves of the meander. At one location, the river doubles back on itself seven times, and flows five to six miles in order to cover one straight line mile.

ACTIVITIES - Camp in the campground open year-round and located at 4,500 feet. Hike the narrow Honaker Trail located 1.5-miles northwest of the Goosenecks. The trail drops 1,200 feet down to the river in 2.5 miles. Another trail leads to Mendenhall Loop and a stone cabin built by an early prospector who processed gold dust into lumps by adding mercury and baking the mixture in a potato.

INFORMATION -
Goosenecks of the San Juan State Park
P.O. Box 48
Blanding, Utah 84511
801-259-8151

SCOFIELD LAKE STATE PARK
5

LOCATION - The park is on Soldier Summit and is three miles north of Scofield off U.S. 6 on Utah 96.

ACTIVITIES - The park is Utah's highest at 7,600 feet. Its lake covers 2,800 acres and is one of the best areas for year-round trout fishing and boating from the ramps or boat slips. Camping facilities include 40 sites open from May 1 to November 30. It has 40 RV sites and 100 tent sites with showers

available. Reservations: P.O. Box 166, Price, Utah 84501-0166, 801-448-9449.
INFORMATION -
Scofield Lake State Park
P.O. Box 166
Price, Utah 84501-0166
801-448-9449

MILLSITE STATE PARK
6

LOCATION - The lake is four miles west of Ferron in central Utah off Utah 10.

ACTIVITIES - Primitive camping is provided for 22 RVs and 12 tents at 6,200 feet. The campground is open year-round. Here you can also picnic, swim, fish and water ski.
INFORMATION -
Millsite State Park
Southeast Region Office
125 West 200 North
Moab, Utah 84532-2330
801-259-8151

HUNTINGTON LAKE STATE PARK
7

LOCATION - The lake is two miles northwest of Huntington off Utah 10.

ACTIVITIES - The park offers water skiing, boating, and swimming in a roped-off swimming area near a nice beach.

The campground at 5,800 feet is open April 1 through November 30. It has sites for 30 RVs and 30 tents with showers available. For reservations: 281 South Main, Orangeville, Utah 84537; 801-748-2342
INFORMATION -
Huntington Lake State Park
P.O. Box 1343
Huntington, Utah 84528-1343
801-748-2342

GREEN RIVER STATE PARK
8

LOCATION - The park is located just off I-70 on the banks of the Green River in the town of Green River.

ACTIVITIES - The Green River is the put-in spot for rafting and float trips. The season begins on Memorial Day with the 180 mile annual "Friendship Cruise" of boats that float from Green River to Moab. Information on float trips is available from the Chamber of Commerce.

The park has 42 campsites. To make campground reservations: Box 93, Green River, Utah 84525, 801-564-3633

For an unusual nearby attraction, travel up to Crystal Geyser, five miles east of Green River, on U.S. 6/50 to I-70, and then seven miles south on a gravel road, to see some unique cold water geyser eruptions occurring twice a day. The water can spurt as high as 100 feet, but the timing of the eruptions is erratic.

INFORMATION -
Green River State Park
P.O. Box 93
Green River, Utah 84525-0093
801-564-3633

GOBLIN VALLEY STATE RESERVE
9

LOCATION - It's 68 miles southwest of Green River via I-70 and Utah 24, or 13 miles north of Hanksville off Utah 24.

FEATURES - The park contains thousands of colorful rock formations of Entrada sandstone forming huge rock goblins.

ACTIVITIES - Picnic, hike, enjoy unlimited off-highway vehicle touring, or camp in the 42 site campground at 4,100 feet. It's open year-round and has 35 RV sites and 20 for tents, along with shower facilities. Reservations are available by writing P.O. Box 81, Green River, Utah 84525-0093. There is no phone available.

Trails north and west of the park go through a stream-cut narrows which barely acccommodate both a hiker and backpack.

A nearby attraction is in Temple Wash, north of the park, where you can see good Indian artwork.

INFORMATION -
Goblin Valley State Reserve

P.O. Box 81
Green River, Utah 84525-0093
No phone

CORAL PINK SAND DUNES STATE PARK
10

LOCATION - 27 miles northwest of Kanab off U.S. 89.

FEATURES - The dunes were created when Navajo sandstone eroded, and then the wind picked up the sand, depositing it into many pink dunes.

ACTIVITIES - The sand dunes offer opportunities for hiking, picnicking, off-road vehicle riding, photography and camping at 6,000 feet. The campground is open April 1 through October 30 and has 22 RV and 22 tent sites plus showers. Reservations for camping: P.O. Box 95, Kanab, Utah 84741-0095.

INFORMATION -
Coral Pink Sand Dunes State Park
P.O. Box 95
Kanab, Utah 84741-0095
602-874-2408

GUNLOCK LAKE STATE PARK
11

LOCATION - The lake is 16 miles northwest of Saint George on Utah 18.

ACTIVITIES - Water sports are available on the reservoir located at 3,600 feet. It also has a swimming pool in the park.

Campground reservations: Box 140, Santa Clara, Utah 84765. No phone available.

INFORMATION -
Gunlock Lake State Park
Box 140
Santa Clara, Utah 84765
No phone

SNOW CANYON STATE PARK
12

LOCATION - Five miles northwest of St. George on Utah 18.

ACTIVITIES - The park is a favorite for camping at 3,400 feet. The campground has showers and is open year-round with 14 RV and 19 tent sites. Campground reservations: P.O Box 140, Santa Clara, Utah 84765-0410; 801-628-2255.

Several extinct volcanic cones are located at the head of the canyon which produced molten lava covering sections of the red sandstone with a black mantle. Visitors will enjoy taking pictures and hiking among the lava and sandstone formations.

INFORMATION -
Snow Canyon State Park
P.O. Box 140
Santa Clara, Utah 84765-0140
801-628-2255

ESCALANTE PETRIFIED FOREST STATE RESERVE
13

LOCATION - One mile west of Escalante on Utah 12.

FEATURES - The park has deposits of colorful mineralized wood along with some dinosaur bones.

ACTIVITIES - Wide Hollow Reservoir is inside the park and offers water sports and fishing. Year-round camping is available at 3,400 feet. It has 14 RV and 22 tent spots. Showers are available. Campground reservations: P.O. Box 350, Escalante, 84726-0350, 801-829-3838. You can also picnic, hike, or tour the visitor center.

INFORMATION -
Escalante Petrified Forest State Reserve
P.O. Box 350
Escalante, Utah 84726-0350
801-829-3838

KODACHROME STATE PARK
14

LOCATION - The park is four miles south of Cannonville off Utah 12 near Bryce Canyon National Park.

ACTIVITIES - The park has some huge limestone formations which resemble gigantic chimneys.

Camp at 5,800 feet from April through November in one of 24 RV and 24 tent sites with shower facilities. For campground reservations: P.O. Box 238, Cannonville, Utah 84718-1238; 801-679-8562.

Stop by the visitor center. Visit the world's only "petrified" geyser hole. Hike the three-eighths of a mile nature trail, enjoy great photography opportunities or go touring in off-highway vehicles.

Nearby attractions include Bryce Canyon National Park, Grosvenor Arch, Paria Canyon, and some movie sets and ghost town remnants.

INFORMATION -
Kodachrome State Park
P.O. Box 238
Cannonville, Utah 84718
801-679-8562

IRON MISSION STATE PARK
15

LOCATION - Cedar City, northwest of the Coal Creek Bridge on Utah 91.

FEATURES - The park is the site of the first iron foundry built west of the Mississippi.

ACTIVITIES - Walk through the horse-drawn vehicle collection which includes vintage stagecoaches and surreys, antique farm machinery, and an original Studebaker white top wagon. You can also see many implements used by the early pioneers who settled the area in the middle 1800s.

While in Cedar City, attend the Shakespeare festival on the South Utah State College campus. Three plays are presented in an open air theater. Matinees are offered at 2:00 P.M. on Wednesday and Saturday, with 8:30 P.M. performances presented Monday and Saturday. The festival runs from mid-July through the end of August. Reservations are advised. Call 801-586-7878 after April 1.

INFORMATION -
Iron Mission State Park
%Southwest Region Office

P.O. Box 1079
Cedar City, Utah 84720-1079
801-586-4497
   or
801-586-9290

ANTELOPE ISLAND STATE PARK
16

LOCATION - The park is located near Salt Lake City in the middle of the Great Salt Lake, eight miles west of Clearfield or via Exit 335 off I-15.

ACCESS - An island ferry operates during the summer. The road that once linked the island with the mainland was flooded in 1980.

FEATURES - Antelope Island is Utah's second largest state park and was named for the antelope that once roamed the area.

ACTIVITIES - You can enjoy camping at 4,200 feet year-round. Reservations: Antelope Island, 4528 West 1700 South, Syracuse, Utah 84041-6861; 801-533-5127.

The area also offers swimming, picnicking, hiking, salt water bathing, "floating" in the dense salt water and canoeing. You can sign up for overnight horseback trips and visit the buffalo herd sanctuary. Egg Island is also in the park where thousands of sea gulls nest annually.

INFORMATION -
Antelope Island
4528 West 1700 South
Syracuse, Utah 84041-6861
801-533-5127 (Northern Region Office)

PIONEER TRAIL STATE PARK
17

LOCATION - Near the mouth of Emigration Canyon at 2601 Sunnyside Avenue in Salt Lake City.

ACTIVITIES - Attend the audio-visual display in the visitor center explaining the trek of the early pioneers from Nauvoo, Illinois, to Salt Lake City. Walk around "This is the Place Monument," erected in 1947 to commemorate the 100th anniversary of the Mormon pioneers' arrival following their 2,000-mile trek.

Walk through the old Deseret Village to see homes of some of the early pioneers, to see how life was lived from 1847 until 1869 when the railroad ended the pioneer era. Go through Brigham Young's farm home. Guided tours: 801-533-5881. If you're lucky, perhaps you can hear one of the descendants of the original settlers give some wonderful details of the pioneers' lives.

From Memorial Day through Labor Day, take a ride aboard a wagon train to enjoy supper along the historic Mormon Trail. Departures are at 6:30 P.M. and reservations are required: 801-583-3190.

While in Salt Lake, tour historic Temple Square where free organ recitals are given Monday-Friday at 12-12:30, and on Saturday and Sunday from 4:00-4:30 P.M. Attend the rehearsal of the well-known 350 voice Tabernacle Choir held on Thursday from 8-9:30 P.M., or their regular broadcast on Sunday from 9:30-10:00 A.M. Plan to be seated by 9:15. Additional free concerts are also offered Friday and Saturday at 7:30 P.M. in the Assembly Hall.

INFORMATION -
Pioneer Trail State Park
% Utah Parks and Recreation
1636 West North Temple, Suite 116
Salt Lake City, Utah 84116-3156
801-533-6011

GREAT SALT LAKE SALTAIR BEACH STATE PARK
18

LOCATION - Sixteen miles west of Salt Lake City on I-80.

ACTIVITIES - Enjoy saltwater bathing, sailing, camping, fishing, rent a water trike, take a power boat cruise on the lake, or go swimming in America's inland sea. Concession stands are located by the former Saltair resort which was destroyed in 1984 by a storm. Camping reservations are accepted. Contact the Northern Region Office in Salt Lake City: 801-533-5127

INFORMATION -
Great Salt Lake Saltair Beach State Park
P.O. Box 323
Magna, Utah 84044-0323
801-533-5127

EAST CANYON LAKE STATE PARK
19

LOCATION - The park is 18 miles south of Morgan. It's also accessible from Ogden or Salt Lake City via I-80/84 and Highway 65/66.

ACTIVITIES - The lake offers good trout fishing, boating and other water sports. Boat rentals and refreshments are available during the summer.

The campground at 5,700 feet is open year-round with 31 RV sites and 300 tent sites. Drinking water is available. Reservations: P.O. Box 97, Morgan, Utah 84050; 801-829-3838.

You can also picnic, hike, boat, swim and fish for trout in this high mountain lake.

INFORMATION -
East Canyon Lake State Park
P.O. Box 97
Morgan, Utah 84050-0097
801-829-3838

WILLARD BAY STATE PARK
20

LOCATION - One park is at the North Marina, 20 miles north of Ogden on I-15 at Exit 360, and the other is at the South Marina, 15 miles north of Ogden on I-15 at Exit 354.

FEATURES - The park is a man-made body of fresh water which has been reclaimed from the salt marshes of the Great Salt Lake. Weather from May through September is generally warm, dry and sunny.

ACTIVITIES - Bird watchers will love this area in which over 200 species have been observed.

Camp in one of 40 RV sites or 12 tent sites complete with picnic tables and drinking water. Reservations: P.O. Box 319, Willard, Utah 84340-0319, 801-723-2694. You can also enjoy boating, sailing, water skiing and year-round fishing. Small boat rentals, food, camping and boating supplies are sold here.

INFORMATION -
Willard Bay State Park
P.O. Box 319
Willard, Utah 84340-0319
801-723-2694

FORT BUENAVENTURA STATE PARK
21

LOCATION - The park is in Ogden at 2450 A. Street.

FEATURES - This was the first Anglo settlement in the Great Basin. The stockade is a replica of trapper Mike Goodyear's fort, which operated from 1843-47.

ACTIVITIES - Open for day use only, you can go canoeing, enjoy a picnic, tour the pioneer cabins, and watch mountain men events.

INFORMATION -
Fort Buenaventura State Park
2450 A Street
Ogden, Utah 84401
801-533-5127

ROCKPORT LAKE STATE PARK
22

LOCATION - Four miles south of Wanship off I-80.

ACTIVITIES - Camp at 6,000 feet in one of the 74 sites from April through November. Reservations: Box 457, Peoa, Utah 84061-0457, 801-336-2241.

The area is a prime water recreation area where you can go boating, swimming, sailboarding or enjoy year round fishing. You can also rent one of the housekeeping cabins.

INFORMATION -
Rockport Lake State Park
P.O. Box 457
Peoa, Utah 84061-0457
801-336-2241

DEER CREEK STATE PARK
23

LOCATION - Take U.S. 189 to Deer Creek Reservoir five miles southwest of Heber City.

ACTIVITIES - Camp at 5,400 feet from April-November in one of 23 sites. Reservations: Box 257, Midway, Utah 84049-0257. You can also enjoy picnicking, year-round fishing, water skiing, sea sledding, sailing, sailboarding, swimming and boating. For boating reservations at Deer Creek Island Resort:

801-654-2155.

For novices wishing to learn to sail or sailboard, contact the Mistral Certified School at 801-654-2136.

INFORMATION -
Deer Creek State Park
P.O. Box 257
Midway, Utah 84049-0257
801-489-7754

WASATCH MOUNTAIN STATE PARK
24

LOCATION - Two miles northwest of Midway off U.S. 40/89.

FEATURES - This is Utah's largest state park. The town of Midway was named when the early pioneers, threatened by Indians in the 1800s, built a fort between their two settlements. Because of its elevation, the summer nights are cool.

ACTIVITIES - See the gold camp, picnic, hike, fish, horseback ride or enjoy the 27 hole golf course. To reserve a tee-off time or for information: 801-654-1791. Food service is available at the Wasatch Park Cafe in the clubhouse.

You can also camp at 5,600 feet from April-November in one of 152 RV sites or 40 tent sites, complete with showers and drinking water. For campground reservations: P.O. Box 218, Midway, Utah 84049-0010, or call 801-363-3232 or 328-2111. Reservations for the Pine Creek Campground may be made by calling 801-654-3961 or 654-0540.

The park also has a large 100 person capacity ranch-type building available for use by campers. Bring your own sleeping equipment and cooking and eating utensils. Reservations: 801-654-0540.

For a nearby attraction, enjoy one of two hot springs located in Midway. The Homestead Hot Springs is at 700 North Homestead Drive, and Mountain Spaa Resort is at 800 North 200 E.

In Heber City, ride the Heber Creeper, a train powered by a steam engine that goes from Heber City past the gorges of Provo Canyon and Bridal Veil Falls to Vivian Park. The train depot is on the western edge of town, six blocks west of Main via 100 South. Information: 801-654-3229. Reservations: 654-2900 in Heber City, or 531-6022 in Salt Lake City.

If you're in town in July, attend the Lambfest Barbeque or the Wasatch County Fair held in August.

Pilots can land at Heber Valley, south of Heber on U.S. 189.

INFORMATION -
Wasatch Mountain State Park
P.O. Box 10
Midway, Utah 84049
801-654-1791

BEAR LAKE RENDEZVOUS BEACH STATE PARK
25

LOCATION - Two miles north of Laketown on Utah 30 or 1.5-miles north of Garden City on U.S. 89.

FEATURES - Bear Lake is 20 miles long and seven miles wide and is Utah's second largest freshwater lake. The area is well known for raspberries which come into season the last of July and first of August.

ACTIVITIES - The campground is at 5,900 feet and is open from May-November. It has 138 sites. For reservations: Box 99, Garden City, Utah 84028; 801-946-3208.

You can also picnic, swim from its large sandy beach, waterski, fish for mackinaw trout and native cutthroat or enjoy small craft activity. The park has a marina, and sailboat regattas are held during the summer.

During the winter, the lake is famous for its annual wintertime run of small "cisco" fish.

At Sweetwater Resort, you can enjoy horseback riding, sailing, water skiing, rowing your own boat or renting a speedboat.

INFORMATION -
Bear Lake Rendezvous Beach State Park
P.O. Box 184
Garden City, Utah 84028-0184
801-946-3208

YUBA LAKE STATE PARK
26

LOCATION - The 14 mile long lake is 25 miles south of Nephi off I-15.

ACTIVITIES - The park is at 6,000 feet, and is open all year for picnicking, boating, swimming, water skiing, year-round fishing for walleye or yellow perch and camping in one of its 19 campsites with showers. Reservations: Box 88, Levan, Utah 84639-0088; 801-489-7754

INFORMATION -
Yuba Lake State Park
P.O. Box 88
Levan, Utah 84639-0088
801-489-7754

STEINAKER LAKE STATE PARK
27

LOCATION - North of Vernal off U.S. 191.
ACTIVITIES - Fish for rainbow trout and bass. Enjoy boating and camping.
INFORMATION -
Steinaker Lake State Park
Steinaker Lake 4335
Vernal, Utah 84078
801-489-7754

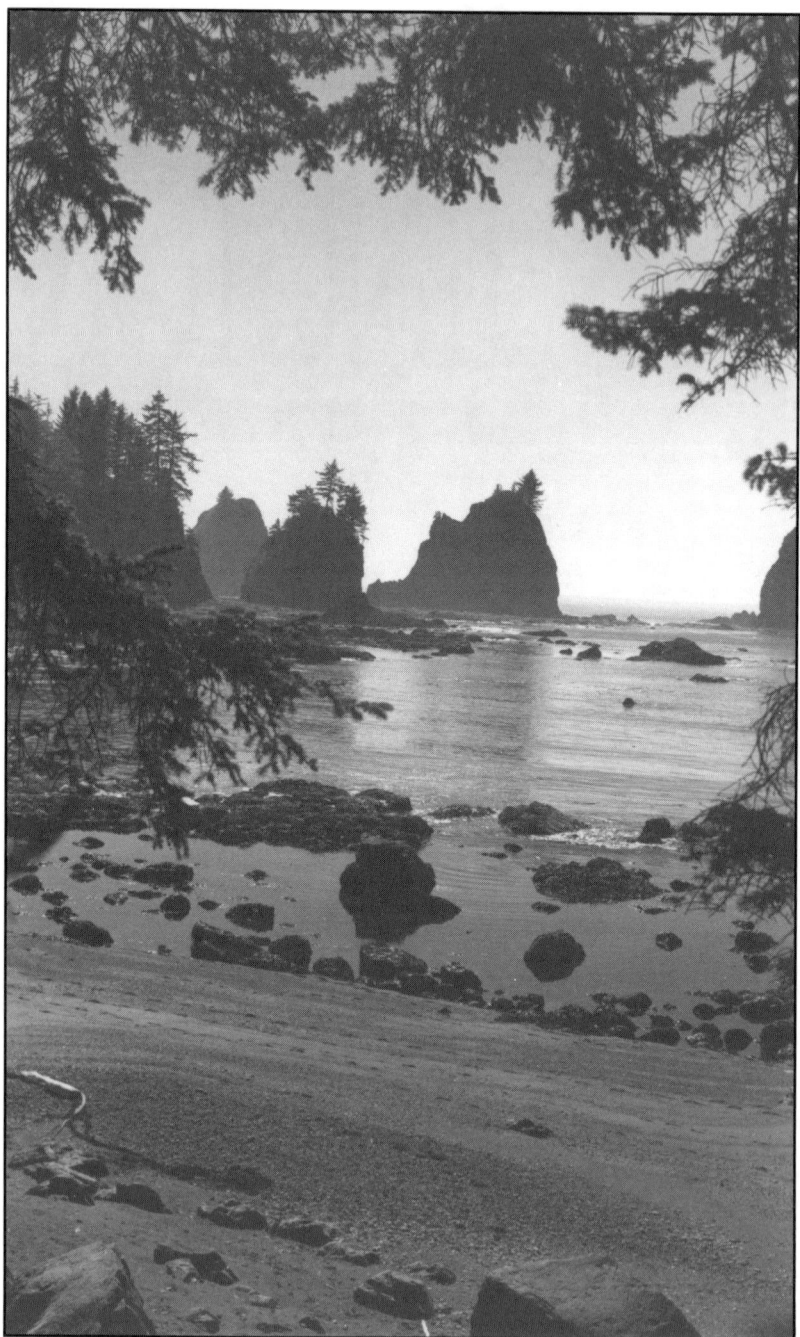

Washington's rugged coast.
OLYMPIC NATIONAL PARK

WASHINGTON

Washington has over 100 state parks, so only a representative selection are included in this guide. The state is a study in contrasts with its flat, green valleys, a rain forest, two mountain ranges — the Olympics and the Cascades, rushing rivers, and even small islands up in the north. As a result, you have an interesting array of activities to select from as well as a wide variation in weather.

GINKGO PETRIFIED FOREST STATE PARK
1

LOCATION - The park is off I-90 at Vantage, Washington. To reach the park, leave I-90 at Exit 136 at Vantage and drive north one mile on Vantage Highway, Washington 10, to the park museum/visitor center. The park is 29 miles east of Ellensburg. It's open from 6:30 A.M. until 10:00 P.M. daily from April 1 to September 30, and from 8-5 the rest of the year.

FEATURES - More than 200 species of trees have been found here. One of these trees, the ginkgo, is a prehistoric North American shade tree, and this is the only place they grew. Authorities believe that over 100,000 of them once grew here, but now they're buried in the once molten lava. These trees date back over 15 million years.

ACTIVITIES - Tour the museum where over 50 varieties of petrified trees are on display. The interpretive center is open weekly except on Monday and Tuesday through mid-September. Listen to a 12-minute presentation on the forest's evolution. See Indian petroglyphs which were originally located along the cliffs of the Columbia River. These picture graphics depict hunts, tribal confrontations and religious experiences.

Hike the three-quarter mile interpretive petrified forest trail where you pass 20 fossil logs, some eight feet long. The campground has 50 campsites with

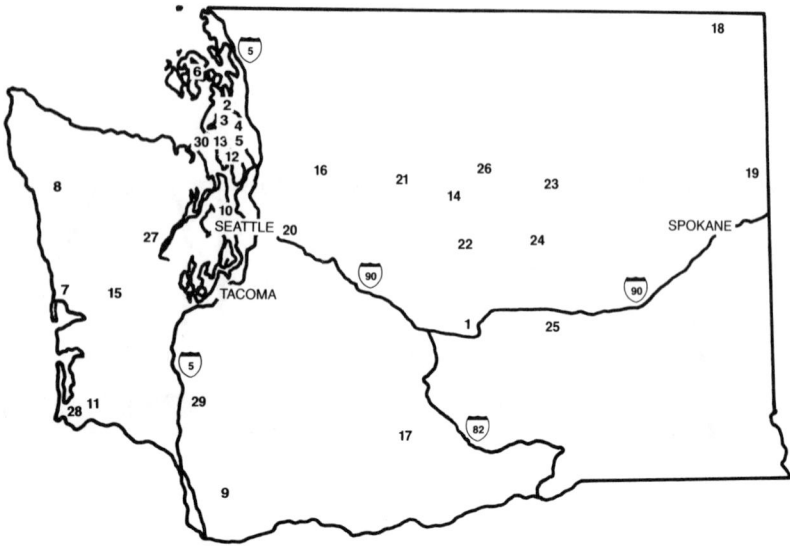

SEATTLE

TACOMA

SPOKANE

18

19

5

6

2
3
4
30 13 5
12
10
27

16

21

26

23

14

22

24

20

90

90

1

25

5

29

17

82

9

7

15

11

28

8

hookups. Visitors can also go fishing, swimming or boating from the boat launch.

At Vantage, enjoy a great view of the Columbia River.

A nearby attraction is Wanapum Lake, a recreation area five miles south of Vantage on I-90. Take Exit 137 onto Washington 243. The Rocky Reach Dam at Wenatchee offers tours where you can see fish ladders, a fish viewing room and the powerhouse.

INFORMATION -
Ginkgo Petrified Forest State Park
Vantage, Washington 98950
509-856-2700

DECEPTION PASS
2

LOCATION - Deception Pass State Park is located on both sides of the channel at the northern end of Whidbey Island and is 10 miles north of Oak Harbor on Washington 20 at the confluence of the Juan de Fuca and Rosario straits. If you drive across the Deception Pass Bridge, be sure to stop to get a good look at the roiling water below you.

The park may be reached by ferry from Mukilteo to Columbia Beach on the southeast tip of the island. Then take Highway 20E to the tip of the island, 50 miles away.

Driving access is from the north. Leave I-5 at Exit 230 north of Mount Vernon and take Washington 20 to the east.

Pilots can fly into Oak Harbor Airport located three miles southwest of town.

FEATURES - The pass is an ancient river channel created when the earth's crust gradually rose following the melting of glacial ice. The island is known for its forests, sea life and beaches.

ACTIVITIES - The park has 13 miles of water frontage. Camp in one of 251 sites or in one of the primitive hiker/biker sites, hike, swim in fresh water by a sandy beach, fish for fresh water trout at Pass Lake, rent a boat or scuba dive in the underwater park. Concessions are availalable.

WHIDBEY ISLAND
3

LOCATION - The South Whidbey Island Recreation Area is on the west side of the island, 4.5-miles southwest of Greenbank and 13 miles south of

Coupeville.

ACTIVITIES - Camp in one of 54 sites, picnic, hike in forested Puget Sound or in the Olympic Mountains. You can also beachcomb, fish, swim and go clam digging along the sandy beach.

CORNET BAY
4

LOCATION - The Cornet Bay State Park is near Deception Pass. Go across Deception Pass Bridge onto the island. Then after one mile, turn east onto Cornet Bay and continue for another one and one-quarter miles.

ACTIVITIES - Go boating, have a picnic, fish, bike, scuba dive, hike, beachcomb and go clamming.

Cranberry Lake is also close to Deception Pass. The entrance is three-quarters of a mile south of the bridge on Washington 20. This area has 230 campsites and picnicking facilities. You can swim, go boating, hike or fish for stocked trout.

FORT CASEY STATE PARK
5

LOCATION - Fort Casey is three miles south of Coupeville off Washington 20. Pilots can land at privately-owned Coupeville Airpark, three miles south of the city. Call 206-678-4147 for advance permission.

FEATURES - Fort Casey has some late 19th century fortifications which are still intact. You can see two 10-inch "disappearing guns," possibly the only ones of their size still in existence.

ACTIVITIES - Go camping in one of 35 sites in an historic U.S. Defense Post, picnic, hike, boat from the boat ramp, enjoy good bottom fishing for salmon and steelhead or explore the underwater scuba park.

Tour the Lighthouse Interpretive Center to learn more about the Puget Sound Defense System which operated from 1900-1940. It's open Wednesday-Sunday from 10:00 A.M. to 6:00 P.M. from April 1-September 30.

Coupeville was begun in 1853 and is one of the oldest cities in the state. While in town, drive along Madrona Drive west of town, a four-mile scenic route that goes by Penn Cove. Flower lovers will enjoy being in town in late April when you can attend the Holland Happening and see many colorful tulips in bloom. Be sure to stop by the Holland Gardens and walk through their special display.

INFORMATION -
Fort Casey State Park
206-678-4519
  or
Coupeville Chamber of Commerce
5 South Main Street
Coupeville, Washington 98239
206-678-5434

SAN JUAN ISLANDS
6

LOCATION - The San Juan Islands are 170 islands scattered north of Puget Sound between Canada and the U.S.

ACTIVITIES - The islands are very popular for bicycling. Riders setting out on rides of any length should travel prepared to handle on-the-road repairs, food and water, since there are very few towns on the islands.

When you take the ferry to the San Juans, you only pay when traveling to the west. If you purchase a ticket in Anacortes through to Friday Harbor on San Juan, you can then see the other three islands free while returning to Anacortes. You also travel free if you're going between the islands on foot. Most resorts offer pick-up service from the ferry.

When you ride the ferry, you should arrive at least an hour early since no reservations are accepted. It takes two hours to get to Friday Harbor from Anacortes. To get a ferry schedule, call 800-542-7052 or 800-542-0810.

Private pilots who want flight following as you fly from Whidbey Island en route to the San Juans can contact the Whidbey Island Naval Air Station on 118.2 or 120.7. Charters to the islands are available from Seattle. Contact Lake Union Air at 800-692-9223, or Chart Air at 800-237-1101.

The islands lie in the rain shadow of the Olympic Mountains so winter temperatures are mild, and summer temperatures are in the 70s. Annual precipitation is 18-22 inches.

MORAN STATE PARK
SAN JUAN ISLANDS

LOCATION - Moran State Park is on Orcas Island near Eastsound and is accessible by state ferry or by private aircraft. Pilots can land at Eastsound, one mile north of the city. No taxi service is available, but you can rent a moped: 206-376-2474, or a rental car: 376-4282.

FEATURES - Orcas Island was named for the killer whales who cruise the island in groups called pods.

ACTIVITIES - Mount Constitution, 2,409 feet in elevation, is located on the eastern side of the island. Here you can climb a stone tower on the top for an unrestricted 360-degree look at the San Juan and Gulf Islands, Olympics, Vancouver Island and Mount Baker. If you hike to the top of the mountain, you'll discover several small lakes.

Fresh water fishing is available in the park lakes, where there are also concession stands with boat rentals and fishing supplies.

Camp in one of 136 tent sites. Group camping is available. Information: Star Route, Box 22, Eastsound Washington 98245, 206-376-2326, or call 1-800-562-0990.

Cascade Lake is the location of the park's headquarters and offers picnic facilities, hiking, sailboarding, swimming, boat rentals, showers and trout fishing. A fishing license is required.

Mountain Lake, up the road from Cascade, has 18 campsites. There are 30 miles of hiking trails in this park. One hike goes around Mountain Lake in 3.6-miles. You can then continue on to Twin Lakes on the Mount Constitution trail. You can also hike to Cascade Falls.

If you arrive on the island by bicycle, you'll have 13 hilly miles to ride to reach the park. To reach the top of Mount Constitution involves another five strenuous miles of riding, with an elevation gain of 2,300 feet, but it's well worth the effort. A bicycle shop is located in Eastsound: The Island Chain Saw.

On Orcas, you can also take a kayak cruise. Contact the Orcas Island Kayak Guides, P.O. Box 121, Olga, Washington 98279, or in Doe Bay Village: 206-376-2291.

INFORMATION -
1-800-562-0990
    or
Northwest Tourism Region
Anacortees Chamber of Commerce
917 134th Street S.W.
Everett, Washington 98204
206-742-2200

CATTLE POINT STATE PARK
SAN JUAN ISLANDS

LOCATION - On San Juan Island, the state park is near American Camp on the southeast end of the island.

ACCESS - Access to the island is via state ferry, San Juan Airlines or via private aircraft landing either at Friday Harbor and at Roche Harbor. At Friday Harbor, you can get a taxi: 206-378-3550, a moped: 206-378-5244, or a rental car: 206-378-5545, or in town at the Friday Harbor Motor Inn: 206-378-4351. At Roche Harbor, contact 206-378-2155 for a rental car, or a taxi at 206-378-4711.

FEATURES - The "Pig War" resulted from a dispute between the U.S. and Britain over which country would possess Oregon Country, then consisting of the present states of Washington, Oregon, Idaho, parts of Montana, Wyoming and the Province of British Columbia. In 1846, the Oregon Treaty gave the U.S. possession of the Pacific Northwest south of the 49th parallel and left Great Britain possession of Vancouver Island and all the land to the north of the 49th parallel.

Then in 1859, an American farmer on the island became angry about a British-owned pig rooting in his potato patch and shot him. This led to a military confrontation between the U.S. and Britain with both sides building up their forces. No shots were ever fired, however, and eventually the two sides agreed to joint occupation of San Juan. Twelve years later, the English withdrew from the island.

The island is still remembered for this military confrontation where the only casualty turned out to be a pig.

ACTIVITIES - Tour the earthworks and historic displays on the pig war at American Camp.

Biking in San Juan is hilly and along narrow roads with a lot of traffic. You can rent bikes in Friday Harbor. A bicycling guide, "15 Bike Rides on San Juan Island," may be obtained in the local drug store.

Bicycling laws on San Juan Island provide strict fines for illegally parking your bike, for riding on the sidewalk, not signaling, not riding on the right side of the road or for riding two abreast.

A scenic circle bike ride leaves from Friday Harbor via Bailor Hill Road to the West Side Road which leads to Lime Kiln Park. This road is all paved and has a long climb up Bailor Hill before dropping down to the west side. If you make this into a loop ride, you'll encounter around two miles of hard-packed dirt as you loop back via Roche Harbor Road before reaching pavement once again.

For a good hike, go to Cattle Point where the trail at Jaeckle's Lagoon goes through the woods passing three other lagoons.

American Camp has the longest public beach in the San Juans where you can sunbathe, picnic or enjoy some whale watching. One hour guided historical walks leave from the visitor center around 11:00 A.M. from July 4-Labor Day. You can also watch a re-enactment of soldier life at the camp on weekends from noon to 3:00 P.M. Check with the visitor center for exact details.

Tour the Whale Museum located a few blocks from the ferry at the top of the First Street hill. It's closed Tuesdays.

Attend the San Juan Jazz Festival in July. Information: 206-378-5509. Tickets are available from The San Juan Island Goodtime Classic Jazz Association, P.O. Box 1379, Friday Harbor, Washington 98250. During the festival, a shuttle bus provides transportation from the campgrounds, Roche Harbor, fairgrounds and from downtown. Reservations for accommodations for this festival are mandatory.

Take a wildlife cruise to see the island's resident whale orcas. The ship departs daily except on Tuesday and Thursday at 1:00 P.M. from Port Friday Harbor. Reservations are highly recommended: 206-378-5315.

Scuba divers enjoy looking for the world's largest octopi.

For a sailing cruise, contact the Nor'Wester Charters at Friday Harbor: 206-378-5478 or 883-0302.

The second weekend in September, attend "Weekend with the Classics" to see a display of antique cars, boats and planes.

INFORMATION -
Chamber of Commerce
P.O. Box 98
Friday Harbor, Washington 98250
206-378-4600

LIME KILN STATE PARK
SAN JUAN ISLANDS

LOCATION - On the west side of San Juan.

ACTIVITIES - If your timing is right, you should be able to get a glimpse of the resident orcas who live in the area. They don't migrate long distances and are commonly spotted in the summer as they feed on salmon on their way to breed in the fresh water rivers of Puget Sound. For information on their whereabouts, call the Whale Watch hotline at 1-800-562-8832.

You can also explore the tidal pool and see some historic lime kilns located outside the park boundary.

Guided interpretive talks are offered May-September. For information, contact the park ranger in Friday Harbor.

The park's lighthouse has an automated light and foghorn, but isn't open to the public.

INFORMATION -
Chamber of Commerce
P.O. Box 98
Friday Harbor, Washington 98250
206-378-4600

LOPEZ ISLAND: SPENCER SPIT STATE PARK
SAN JUAN ISLANDS

ACCESS - Access is via state ferry or private aircraft to Lopez Island Airport located three miles south of town. No public transportation is available, but a courtesy car is at the airport.

ACTIVITIES - The long sand spit has a mile long beach along the waterfront, good for walking, beach combing and wading. It also offers good year-round clamming, fishing, swimming, picnicking and primitive campsites for hikers and bikers. Bikers coming to the park will ride five miles from the ferry. For information on the campground, call 206-468-2251. No reservations are accepted, so arrive early. The campground usually fills by noon on the weekend.

Bikers can also stay at the Hummel Haven Bicycle Camp which has 25 campsites. Reservations here are highly recommended during the summer. They also have bike rentals, boat rentals and cabins. Information: 206-468-2217. Bikers can rent bikes from The Islander Lopez: 206-468-2233, or at Island Bicycles: 206-378-4941. For repairs, the Lopez Bicycle Works is available: 206-468-2547.

Odlin State Park is one mile from the ferry. They don't accept reservations for individual bicyclists, but will accept them for groups of ten or more. Reservations: 206-468-2496.

Supplies are available in town at the Richardson General Store.

For good sunset or sunrise watching, go to Shark Reef accessible via a short path from the south end of Shark Reef Road. For a secluded beach, go to Watmough Bay Road at the south end of the island and take the road to the left.

Sail aboard the 50-foot yacht, Harmony, which resembles a Spanish galleon.

Special events: Saltwater Kayak Weekend; Paddle, Peddle 'N Sail Weekend. For information: U.S. Inc., % Doug Fox Travel, Seattle, Washington 206-789-6500.

Here's a new concept: Elderhosteler accommodations. This group sponsors programs for seniors which combine hosteling with education. The programs usually last a week and are offered spring, summer and fall at the Islander Lopez: 206-468-2233.

INFORMATION -
Northwest Region
Anacortes Chamber of Commerce
917 134 Street S.W.
Everett, Washington 98204
206-742-2200

OCEAN CITY STATE PARK
7

LOCATION - The park is located along the Pacific Ocean, two miles north of Ocean Shores on Washington 115.

ACTIVITIES - Picnic facilities and 178 camp sites are located among the pine groves. You'll also find 29 hookups and a trailer dumping facility. Enjoy ocean swimming, surf fishing and excellent clamming, particularly for razor clams. It's best to dig along the surf line at low tide watching for small depressions in the wet sand. You must have a license to clam, and, at one time, you were limited to 15 clams. Salmon fishing charters begin from here.

INFORMATION -
206-289-3553
    or
Olympic Peninsula Tourism Region
Department W
P.O. Box 303
Port Angeles, Washington 98632
206-479-3594

BOGACHIEL STATE PARK
8

LOCATION - Six miles south of Forks on U.S. 101.

ACTIVITIES - The area is popular for fishing for spawning steelhead trout and salmon. You can hike along trails through the thick forest or along the beach.

Camp in one of 41 tent sites or in a primitive hiker/biker site.

INFORMATION -
Olympic Peninsula Tourism Region
Department W
P.O. Box 303
Port Angeles, Washington 98632
206-479-3594

BATTLEGROUND LAKE RECREATION AREA
9

LOCATION - Twenty miles northeast of Vancouver and three miles east on Washington 503.

ACTIVITIES - Camp in one of 50 sites or in the hiker/biker sites, picnic, hike, boat from the boat ramp, enjoy fishing for trout, excellent swimming from the sandy beach, riding along trails to the primitive equestrian camping area and scuba diving. Concessions are available.

INFORMATION -
Southwest Tourism Region
Skamania County Chamber of Commerce
P.O. Box 1037
Stevenson, Washington 98648
206-479-3594

BLAKE ISLAND STATE PARK
10

LOCATION - Eight miles west of Seattle along Puget Sound, the island is only accessible by boat. Tours to the island leave from Pier 56 in Seattle. For reservations: 206-329-5700.

ACTIVITIES - Go clamming, camping in 30 tent and 11 primitive sites plus a few hiker/biker sites, picnic, hike, scuba, fish for bottom fish off the reef, swim and hike the three-quarters of a mile nature trail loop or eight additional miles of hiking trails.

Village concessions are available along with authentic Indian salmon dinners. Watch dancers perform rare Northwest Coast dances.

INFORMATION -
206-947-0905
    or

South Puget Sound Tourism
Thurston County Parks and Recreation
Department W
529 West 4th Avenue
Olympia, Washington 98501
206-786-5595

FORT COLUMBIA STATE PARK
11

LOCATION - Two miles east of Chinook along U.S. 101.

FEATURES - The fort has a military post established at the Columbia River's mouth during the Spanish-American War. It has 30 structures including bunkers, search light stations and eight-inch gun batteries.

ACTIVITIES - For day use only, tour the newly renovated interpretive center housed in a restored barracks building. It contains artifacts from military life at the fort. It's open from mid-June through late September and by appointment the rest of the year.

Tour the art gallery and museum from May 15-September from 9-5.

Take a half-mile self-guided tour past the historic installations or hike up Scarboro Trail.

INFORMATION -
Southwest Tourism Region
Skamania County Chamber of Commerce
P.O. Box 1037
Stevenson, Washington 98648
206-479-3594

FORT FLAGLER STATE PARK
12

LOCATION - The fort is on Marrowstone Island eight miles northeast of Hadlock and 10 miles northeast of Chimacum. It's across from Port Townsend Bay.

FEATURES - The fort was established in 1890 and is part of the coastal defense system known as the Devil's Triangle. It had six 12-inch disappearing guns.

ACTIVITIES - Hike along the various trails that connect the various gun batteries and tour the historic fort.

At Long Beach, you get some great views of Puget Sound and the Cascade Mountains.

Camp along a saltwater beach where you can clam, crab, or go fishing for salmon and bottom fish. Go boating from the boat ramp or enjoy their scuba diving area. Camping is available in 116 tent sites and two primitive sites. The campground has a dumping station, groceries and fishing supplies.

INFORMATION -
206-385-1259
  or
Olympic Peninsula Tourism
Department W
P.O. Box 303
Port Angeles, Washington 98632
206-479-3594

FORT WORDEN STATE PARK
13

LOCATION - One mile north of Port Townsend on Washington 20.

FEATURES - The fort guarded Puget Sound during Theodore Roosevelt's presidency. The Victorian residences along Officers' Row have been restored.

ACTIVITIES - Tour Point Wilson Lighthouse erected in 1870, located on the point of the Strait of Juan de Fuca. It's one of the oldest lighthouses in the area and is open Wednesday-Friday from 1-3, and from 1-4 Saturday and Sunday.

Write for an activity schedule from the Centrum Foundation, P.O. Box 1158, Port Townsend, Washington, 98368.

Go scuba diving, camp in sites with 50 hookups and three primitive sites. Year-round reservations are available. Picnic, go boating from the boat ramp, fish, swim from the swimming beach and tour the visitor center. Food service is available. A lodge with vacation cabins is located in the park.

Attend the rhododendron festival which is held at Port Townsend in May.

INFORMATION -
206-385-4730
  or
Olympic Peninsula
Department W
P.O. Box 303
Port Angeles, Washington 98632
206-479-3594

LAKE CHELAN STATE PARK
14

LOCATION - Nine miles west of Chelan off U.S. 97.

ACTIVITIES - Spring is a good time to visit when you'll be in time for the cherry blossoms. Then the motels usually fill up fast, so reservations are encouraged.

A passenger excursion boat offers round-trip service daily to Stehekin at the north end of the lake. It operates daily from May 15 through October 15, and three times weekly the rest of the year. For information: 509-682-2022.

The park has 151 campsites, 17 with hookups, and two primitive sites. Reservations are accepted from Memorial Day through Labor Day. For information: 509-687-3710

The park is a mecca for water sports with its 55-mile long lake. Enjoy scuba diving, camping, picnicking, hiking, boating from the boat ramp, fishing, swimming, water skiing, sailing, parasailing, wind surfing and riding in a hot air balloon from May-September. Concessions and fishing supplies are available in the park.

The park is a haven for backpackers and mountaineers, since the lake valley is the starting point for many hikes. Hikers generally use the ferry, "Lady of the Lake," which runs from Chelan to Stehekin.

Come to Chelan in July for a week of hang gliding competition in the Chelan Classic. In late July, attend the city's Bach Festival.

INFORMATION -
Chamber of Commerce
1-800-4CHELAN
   or
Route 1, Box 90
Chelan, Washington 98816
509-687-3710

LAKE SYLVIA RECREATION AREA
15

LOCATION - This is a small, forested park, located one mile north of Montesano off U.S 12.

ACTIVITIES - Picnic, walk the hiking trails, and go boating from the boat ramp where boat rentals are available. Enjoy fishing, swimming, camping in one of 35 tent sites or in one of the two primitive sites. Groceries and fishing supplies are available.

INFORMATION -
206-249-3621
or
Southwest Tourism Region
% Skamania County Chamber of Commerce
P.O. Box 1037
Stevenson, Washington 98648
206-479-3594

WALLACE FALLS STATE PARK
16

LOCATION - Two miles northeast of Gold Bar off U.S. 2.
ACTIVITIES - Hike the 2.5-mile trail that drops 880 feet to reach the crest of Wallace Falls.

Enjoy a forest setting for tent camping in six sites located at the trailhead. No RVs are allowed.

INFORMATION -
King County Tourism Region
Seattle-King County Convention and Visitors Bureau
Department W
1815 7th Avenue
Seattle, Washington 98101
206-447-4240

FORT SIMCOE STATE PARK
17

LOCATION - Thirty miles west of Toppenish off I-90, and at the end of Washington 220.
ACTIVITIES - The fort was established in 1856. Today, you can still see several of the original buildings beside the old parade ground. You can also see barracks and blockhouses.

For day use only, the park is a bird watchers' paradise. Take a ranger-led tour during the summer.

You can also hike, picnic under the shady oak trees and tour the interpretative center to learn more about the military history of the area. It's open Wednesday-Sunday from April 1-October 16, and by appointment the rest of the year.

INFORMATION -
Fort Simcoe State Park
509-874-2372 or 662-0420

CRAWFORD STATE PARK
18

LOCATION - Eleven miles northwest of Metaline Falls off Washington 31.

FEATURES - Gardner Cave is the second largest limestone cavern in Washington. The cave was discovered in 1899 and contains calcite deposits which have formed stalactites and stalagmites. It's believed that bootleggers once stashed their goods here during Prohibition.

ACTIVITIES - Take a ranger-led tour between May and mid-September. Camping is available in 10 primitive sites.

INFORMATION -
Northeast Tourism Region
Department W
W. 926 Sprague
Spokane, Washington 99204
509-624-1341

MOUNT SPOKANE STATE PARK
19

LOCATION - Thirty miles northeast of Spokane beyond Washington 206.

ACTIVITIES - Mount Spokane is 5,881 feet high and has good skiing during the winter. In summer you can horseback ride or drive to the summit of the peak. A hiking trail leaves from the end of the road.

Camp in one of 12 tent sites or in one of the two primitive sites. Enjoy a great view from Vista House where you can see four states and Canada. Concessions, resort facilities and a restaurant are available in the park.

INFORMATION -
Northeast Tourism Region
Department W
W. 926 Sprague
Spokane, Washington 99204
509-624-1341

LAKE SAMMAMISH STATE PARK
20

LOCATION - Fifteen miles from Seattle, and 1.5-miles northwest of Issaqua. Take Exit 15 from I-90.

FEATURES - The lake is nine miles long. The town of Issaquah is a former coal mining center and has many restored 19th century buildings.

ACTIVITIES - Open for day use only, the park offers swimming, water skiing, fishing and sandy beaches.

Nearby you can tour a chocolate factory and a salmon hatchery.

Near Bellevue, in the nearby Tiger, Squauk and Couger Mountains, enjoy some great hiking in an area often referred to as the "Issaquah Alps."

INFORMATION -
King County Tourism Region
Seattle-King County Convention and Visitors Bureau
Department W
1815 7th Avenue
Seattle, Washington 98101
206-447-4240

LAKE WENATCHEE
21

LOCATION - Twenty-two miles north of Leavenworth on Washington 207.

ACTIVITIES - Go boating from the boat launch, rent one of their canoes, take a guided horseback ride, camp in one of 200 secluded, wooded campground sites, go windsurfing, hike the trails, or go fishing in Fish Lake where you can try your luck at catching perch, bass or trophy-sized German brown trout.

In the fall, drive through Tumwater Canyon to see the trees change colors.

Take a float trip by contacting Wenatchee Whitewater and Scenic Float Tours: 509-782-2254.

While in the park, take a steep half-mile hike to Hidden Lake. To reach the trailhead, follow the Lake Wenatchee Road to Road #6750 along the southern shore of the lake. The trail begins at the end of the road.

To hike a seven-mile round trip to Heather Lake, take the Lake Wenatchee Road to Little Wenatchee where you turn onto Road #6701. At the next intersection, take Road #400 to reach the trailhead. It's best hiked during the latter part of the summer because of the bogs.

For additional hiking possibilities, get a copy of *Trips and Trails in the Northern Cascades*.

Bikers will enjoy the ride from the state park to the head of the lake where you can stop for brunch. You can also take a loop ride from the state park, past Fish Lake and Thousand Trail Campground into Plain. Return via Washington 209.

You can also ride from Leavenworth to Lake Wenatchee, or from Wenatchee to Lake Chelan. Avoid the Knapps Hill tunnel on the way up. Instead, turn left at Navaree Coulee to go through 25 Mile Creek and Chelan, and return to Wenatchee via Washington 97. You'll pass through the tunnel this time, but it usually only requires a minute to clear since you're going downhill.

Cyclists should carry equipment for fixing flats because of the vines growing along the route that tend to puncture tires. Also the back roads don't offer many amenities, so carry along plenty of food and water.

Special events in Lake Chelan include the Manson Apple Blossom Festival in May, Harvest Festival in September, and a sailing regatta in September.

INFORMATION -
Lake Wenatchee State Park
509-763-3101

LINCOLN ROCK STATE PARK
22

LOCATION - Six miles north of East Wenatchee on Washington 2 between East Wenatchee and Orondo.

ACTIVITIES - Camp in one of 94 sites. To reserve one, contact the state reservations office. You can also go swimming, boating, or try your skill at windsurfing. Covered picnic facilities are available.

INFORMATION -
Wenatchee National Forest
301 Yakima Street
P.O. Box 811
Wenatchee, Washington 98801
509-884-3044

STEAMBOAT LAKE STATE PARK
23

LOCATION - Eight miles south of Grand Coulee on Washington 155, near Grand Coulee Dam.

FEATURES - Steamboat Rock is 800 feet tall and 2.5-miles long. A dry coulee is located in the old channel of the Columbia River at Banks Lake. Geologists believe that the basalt rock formation was once located between two huge waterfalls.

ACTIVITIES - Go swimming from the beach, boating from the boat launch, water skiing, fishing in Banks Lake all year-round, or reserve one of the campsites complete with 100 hookups. Horseback riding trails are located in nearby Northrup Canyon.

Nearby Grand Coulee Dam is one of the largest hydroelectric dams and the largest concrete structure in the world. It's particularly spectacular when the spillway is lit at night.

INFORMATION -
Steamboat Lake State Park
509-633-1304

SUN LAKES STATE PARK
24

LOCATION - The park is six miles south of Coulee City on Washington 17, and 17 miles north of Soap Lake.

FEATURES - Dry Falls, north of Sun Lakes, is a crater 3.5-miles wide and 400 feet deep. The falls were left high and dry centuries ago when the Columbia River changed its course.

ACTIVITIES - The park includes several lakes: Park, Coulee, Blue, Alkali, Lenore, and Soap Lake. Enjoy sandy beaches, hiking, horseback riding, stagecoach rides, evening hayrides, cookouts and good fishing for trout, bass and crappie.

The campground has 209 sites and 18 with hookups. There is an 18-hole golf course plus 64 cabins available for rent in the park. For information: 509-632-5291.

In mid-July, attend or compete in the Great Canoe Race from Sun Lake to Soap Lake. The course covers five lakes. Categories include a two-person marathon, a 10-person relay, or an "iron person" who does it all. For information: 509-246-1281.

Soap Lake is believed to have medicinal properties, and thousands come here annually to bathe in the lake and to coat themselves with mud. The lake has 16 natural chemicals.

Nearby, explore the caves of Lake Lenore, carved by Ice Age upheavals.

Take a float trip or go river rafting with Wenatchee Whitewater and Scenic Floats: 509-782-2254.

INFORMATION -
Sun Lakes State Park
300 Beach Street E
Soap Lake, Washington 98851
509-246-1821 or 632-5583

POTHOLES RECREATION AREA
25

LOCATION - Twenty-five miles southwest of Moses Lake on Washington 170.

ACTIVITIES - The area has excellent fishing for trout, walleye, perch and crappie. Camp in one of 126 campsites with 60 hookups and trailer dumping available. Go waterskiing, boating or bird watching. 214 different species have been spotted here.

Rent a boat and stake a claim on your own sandy island. The 50 nearby lakes are filled with trout.

INFORMATION -
Potholes Recreation Area
509-765-7271

ALTA LAKE STATE PARK
26

LOCATION - Two miles southwest of Pateros off Washington 153.

ACTIVITIES - Fish, waterski, swim or camp in one of 200 campsites, 16 complete with hookups. Go boating or hike the one-mile trail that leads to a scenic overlook.

INFORMATION -
Alta Lake State Park
509-923-2473

LAKE CUSHMAN STATE PARK
27

LOCATION - Seven miles west of Hoodsport on the Lake Cushman Road.

ACTIVITIES - The park is located along ten miles of a man-made lake surrounded by the Olympic Mountains.

Enjoy trout fishing, swimming, boating and picnicking. Camp in one of 80 campsites or in one of the primitive hiker/biker sites. The park serves as a base camp for backpacking into the Olympics.

INFORMATION -
Lake Cushman State Park
206-877-5491

FORT CANBY STATE PARK
28

LOCATION - Near Astoria on the Long Beach peninsula, the park is 2.5-miles southwest of Ilwaco off U.S. 101 at the tip of Cape Disappointment.

ACTIVITIES - The park is open from April through October. The campground has 250 sites with 60 hookups. Reservations are necessary: P.O. Box 488, Ilwaco, Washington 98624, 206-753-5755.

Tour the interpretive center three miles southwest of U.S. 101 on the tip of Cape Disappointment. Exhibits trace the 8,000- mile exploratory trip led by Lewis and Clark. Attend the multi-media presentation telling about their journey.

North of the park is a strip of coastline referred to as the "Graveyard of the Pacific" where at least 250 ships have been wrecked. The most recent was the Troller Carlina in 1978. Because of this dangerous water, a lighthouse was built here in 1856. It's still manned around the clock by the Coast Guard.

Swimming along the beach is not recommended because of the dangerous currents and cold water. There is a protected swimming area located at the campground.

Walkers are treated to 28 miles of hiking along the beach beginning from the North Head Lighthouse to Leadbetter Point. Many trails leave Leadbetter to traverse the dunes and go through the woods. If you go to Leadbetter, you can see a sand dune reserve, marshes, woodlands and an area that's home to over 100 species of birds.

Ilwaco is one of the coast's best deep water fishing ports. You can do some great surf fishing off the north jetty by the Coast Guard Station. The salmon season is June 28 through September 24. You can also fish for sturgeon, tuna and bottom fish.

The constantly blowing wind results in ideal kite flying weather. The record kite flown here was a five-by-six foot parafoil which was kept up for 180 hours and 17 minutes. Still another record was 179 kites flown from a single string.

The area has two golf courses. Ilwaco's Heritage Museum features an authentic, old-time railroad depot.

Drive 4.1-miles across the Columbia River Bridge from Megler to Astoria, or past the cranberry bog to see a sea of red cranberries.

Walk through Oysterville, once the county seat. Now it's listed on the National Register.

Special events in Ilwaco include the Daytime Ragtime Jazz Festival in April, the world's longest beach run in June, a sand sculpturing contest in July, the Ilwaco Salmon Fishing Derby in July and August, the Washington State International Kite Festival in August, and the cranberry festival in October.

INFORMATION -
Fort Canby State Park
206-642-3029

SEAQUEST RECREATION AREA AND MOUNT SAINT HELENS NATIONAL VOLCANIC MONUMENT
29

LOCATION - The park is five miles east of Castle Rock. Take I-5 to Exit 49 and follow Washington 504 to reach the lake.

ACTIVITIES - Camp in the campground with 70 sites, including 16 hookups. It's located near Silver Lake which is considered one of Washington's best spots for bass fishing.

Be sure to tour around the Mount St. Helens Monument to see the results of the 1980 eruption. Slides and information regarding the eruption are presented at the visitor center in Lewis and Clark State Park, south of U.S. 12 off I-5, Exit 68. An even newer visitor center opened in Seaquest State Park in 1986, so you can also stop by here for up-to-date information on the volcano.

If there's any way to arrange for a flight in a chartered plane over the volcano, you'll have an unforgettable view of the devastation left behind. Charters leave from many of the surrounding airports as well as from Seattle. Contact a flight service station on the airport field for further information.

INFORMATION -
Mount St. Helens National Volcanic Monument
Amboy, Washington
206-247-5473

SEQUIM BAY RECREATION AREA
30

LOCATION - The recreation area is located four miles east of Sequim on U.S. 101, then three more miles north on Kitchen Road. Sequim is located in the rain shadow of the Olympics, and despite the fact that the nearby rain forests get 120 inches of annual precipitation, Sequim only gets 16 inches. Ironically it's one of the driest Pacific Coast areas north of San Francisco.

ACTIVITIES - Hike six miles along Dungeness Spit, the longest natural sand jetty in the world, to tour the lighthouse at the end of the spit.

INFORMATION -
Sequim Bay Recreation Area
206-753-9467

*If you like the West at its most rugged, there are
rodeos all summer long in Wyoming.*

WYOMING TRAVEL COMMISSION

WYOMING

Wyoming has 10 state parks and one state recreation area. Walkers can pick up maps for a volksmarch in each of the state parks. The trails are 6.2-miles long, and, as you complete each course, you'll receive a medallion with the individual state park's bar.

Information on all the state parks is available through the Wyoming Recreation Commission, 604 East 25th Street, Cheyenne, Wyoming 82002.

BUFFALO BILL DAM AND STATE PARK
1

LOCATION - Six miles west of Cody on U.S. 14-16-20, the park is an hour's drive from the east gate of Yellowstone National Park.

FEATURES - William F. "Buffalo Bill" Cody is reported to have single-handedly killed more than 4,000 buffalo over an eight-month period to feed the workers who were building the Kansas Pacific Railroad. At age 37, he began his world-touring Buffalo Bill's Wild West Exhibition.

The park preserves Cody's original ranch home, mammoth barn and other buildings. You'll see fascinating memorabilia from his frontier and show days.

The lake has 31 miles of shoreline, and its dam, constructed in 1910, is listed on the National Register of Historic Places. It was the first concrete dam constructed by the Bureau of Reclamation. Today, it's used as a model for arch type dams all over the world.

ACTIVITIES - The park is open from April through October and is a favorite stopping place for travelers en route to Yellowstone National Park.

Buffalo Bill Reservoir offers you excellent trout fishing both summer and fall. The park has a commercial marina from which visitors can go boating, kayaking and canoeing as well as enjoy outstanding windsurfing. For windsurfing lessons, contact Alpine Windsurfing in Cody: 307-587-4460, or Sunlight Sports: 307-587-9517. The Wild West Classic Windsurfing

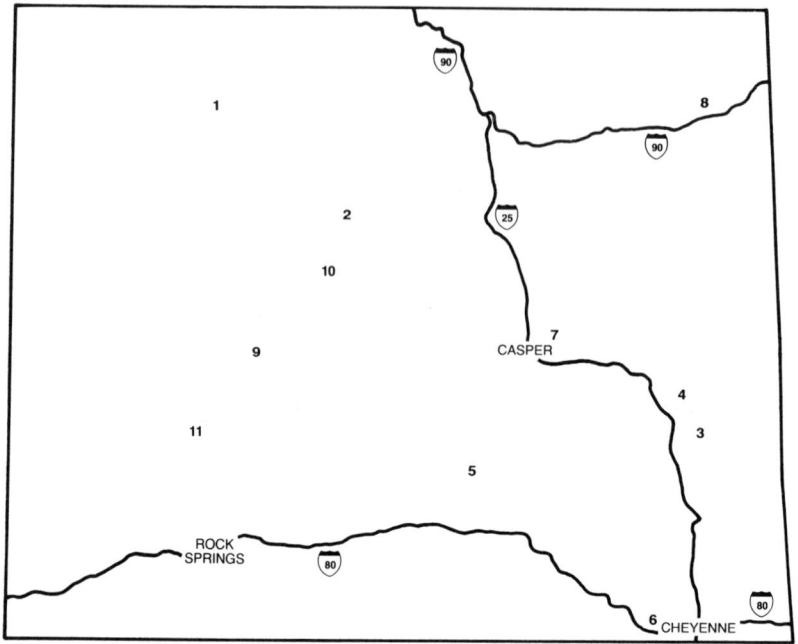

competition takes place at the end of June.

For a river float on the Shoshone River, contact River Runners: 307-527-7238; Rapid Transit: 307-587-3535; or Wyoming River Trips: 307-587-6661.

If you'd like to see other Cody memoriabilia along with artifacts from other early settlers, browse through four museums in the Western Heritage Center near the park. The museums include the Buffalo Bill Museum, Whitney Gallery of Western Art, Plains Indians Museum, and the Winchester Museum. Closed during the winter, they're open daily during the summer, with more limited hours during the spring and fall. For information: 307-587-9227.

Walk through Old Trail Town, a preserved authentic frontier town dating back to the late 1800s, containing a collection of original buildings from all over Wyoming.

Across from the ranch, attend a professional rodeo similar to those Buffalo Bill once participated in. The rodeo is staged nightly beginning at 8:30 starting the latter part of June and continuing through late August. The Cody Stampede is held over the July 4th holiday.

Cody Regional Airport serves pilots and has rental cars from Hertz and Avis.

INFORMATION -
Buffalo Bill Dam and State Park
Cody Chamber of Commerce
P. O. Box 2777
Cody, Wyoming 82414
307-587-2297

HOT SPRINGS STATE PARK
2

LOCATION - The park is on the Big Horn River, east of Thermopolis, on Park Road.

FEATURES - Here you'll find the world's largest mineral hot springs, with water temperatures of 135 degrees. The hot springs have formed beautiful terraces and mineral cones similar to those found in Yellowstone National Park. Watch for a herd of buffalo in the red hills behind the park. Since the animals can be dangerous, it's recommended that you remain in your vehicle.

ACTIVITIES - The Hot Springs Mineral Pools are housed under the large golden dome in the park, and have an indoor, 161-foot water slide. You can soak in a hot pool with a temperature of 105 degrees, swim in either the outdoor or indoor pool, relax in the steam sauna, or have a snack. The facility is open year-round and they rent swimsuits and towels.

Soak for free in the state bathhouse located between two commercial pools. It offers both private bathtubs and a central shallow soaking pool with water temperatures around 104 degrees.

The first part of August, attend the Gift of the Waters Pageant, celebrating the sale of the Hot Springs to the U.S. by the Shoshone and Arapahoe Indians. Events include parades, Indian dancing plus other entertainment. Triathletes can compete in a triathlon which has a 4.8-mile bike leg to the Wedding of the Waters in Wind River Canyon, then a canoe race down the Big Horn River to Hot Springs State Park, finishing with a 4.2-mile run through the park. For details, contact the Chamber of Commerce.

The 10K volksmarch begins from the bathhouse and is the only walk operated year-round. It winds through the park plus a section of downtown Thermopolis. Maps are available at the bathhouse.

Thermopolis holds a Railroad Days celebration in June featuring an arts and crafts show, hobo stew and costume contest, Wildcat Band Carnival, a parade and a poker run. In this unusual competition, players ride horses through downtown, stopping at each tavern along the way for an additional playing card. The one with the best poker hand at the end of the ride wins. For additional information, contact the Chamber of Commerce at 307-864-3192.

History buffs can tour the Hot Springs Museum at 700 Broadway to see a display of pioneer memorabilia including cowboy and oilfield equipment.

Anglers will enjoy some great trout fishing in the Big Horn River, particularly below the Wedding of the Waters at the edge of the Wind River Canyon. Several public fishing areas are located northeast of Thermopolis.

Pilots can land at Thermopolis Airport north of town.

INFORMATION -
Hot Springs State Park
220 Park Street
Thermoplis, Wyoming 82443
307-864-2176

GUERNSEY STATE PARK
3

LOCATION - Along the Platte River off U.S. 26, one mile north of Guernsey.

ACTIVITIES - High bluffs above the lake shield the water from the wind, making it inviting for swimming. With a 27-mile shore line, water skiers have lots of room to explore. Boat rentals are available in town at Quick Canoe and Boat Rentals: 307-836-2039. Jet ski races and a fishing derby are held in mid-June.

There is a collection of historic 1930 Civil Conservation Corps structures located throughout the park. Tour the museum, which required 6,100 man hours to construct, to learn more about the C.C.C. era. The museum opens on May 15th and closes after the Labor Day weekend. For information about special speakers or activities, call 307-836-2900.

The park surrounds a very scenic lake and has 142 camping spots situated around it. Two of the prettiest ones along the paved road are at Red Cloud and Black Canyon Point. The campground only has water and pit toilets. Various additional campsites are located in alcoves and inlets all along the lake.

If you want to camp with hookups, go into the town of Guernsey and camp at Larson's Park along the road to the Oregon Trail Ruts State Historic Site. This campground also has a nine-hole golf course.

Pick up a trail guide and hike the 10K volksmarch in the park from the visitors' center. The trail involves two loops, with one passing near an overlook of the dam, while the other takes you through flower-laden meadows.

The paved park road is very narrow, and bicycling could be quite hazardous.

Take a float trip down the Big Horn beginning either at the Wedding of the Waters and exiting in Thermopolis, or beginning at the Harvey Public Fishing Area 4.5 miles downstream from Thermopolis and exiting near Black Mountain Road, approximately six miles downstream.

The park's season runs from mid-May through the Labor Day weekend. Annual events held here include speed boat races, and a "Guernsey Beach Day" at Sandy Beach.

Wildlife inhabiting the park include deer, antelope, bald eagles, wild turkeys and part of the state's buffalo herd.

The Oregon Trail Ruts are .4 mile south of town from the intersection of Wyoming Avenue. Hike the short trail up to the ruts carved in the sandstone by thousands of covered wagons and oxen-drawn carts as they crossed through here in the mid-1800's.

Continue another 1.8 miles south from the Oregon Trail Ruts to see Register Cliff State Historic Site. Thousands of emigrants wrote their names, dates, place or origin and destination in the soft sandstone as they traveled west.

In Guernsey, the Old Timers Rodeo is held over the Fourth of July, with another rodeo held on Labor Day. Marathoners and shorter distance runners can compete in races held the last Sunday in June.

INFORMATION -
Guernsey State Park
P.O. Box 429
Guernsey, Wyoming 82214
307-836-2334

GLENDO STATE PARK
4

LOCATION - Four miles east of Glendo, northwest of Guernsey State Park, and 28 miles southeast of Douglass on I-25.

ACTIVITIES - The park is open from May through mid-October. Enjoy camping with RV facilities available or stay in your choice of cabins or motel. Campers are advised to arrive early on the weekends since the park receives heavy use. You'll have better luck in securing a campsite during the week.

You can picnic, go hiking, water skiing or boating from the marina. The park boasts great fishing for warm water fish including walleye, perch and catfish.

Go rock hunting for jade, agate, crystal, jasper, onyx and quartzite. Check at the park headquarters for guided rock and fossil hunts.

The 10K volksmarch begins at the Glendo Marina and involves walking two loops through some hilly meadows. The second loop passes the power plant overlook and travels along the bluffs that border the North Platte River. There are several good hills en route, so allow ample time for completion.

Annual events in the park include a walleye fishing tournament held in June, a sail boat regatta, Glendo Days celebration featuring a rodeo and street dance, and the Hobie Cat Regatta in July.

INFORMATION -
Glendo State Park
P.O. Box 398
Glendo, Wyoming 82213
307-735-4433

SEMINOE STATE PARK
5

LOCATION - Thirty-four miles north of Sinclair on Wyoming 351. During the summer access is possible via a county dirt road south out of Alcova.

ACTIVITIES - The park is surrounded by huge white sand dunes, where artifacts dating back 8,000 years have been found. It has two campgrounds with 47 trailer sites at the north end of the reservoir. Enjoy fishing for large trout and walleye in the Seminoe Reservoir.

Boating ramps are located both in the North and South Red Hills areas. Gas and provisions are available at the Seminoe Boat Club at the south end of the park.

This park is close to the "Miracle Mile" stretch of the North Platte where "blue ribbon" fishing, especially for trout, is available. This section of the river is reached by following the county road along the west edge of the reservoir to the area between Pathfinder Reservoir and Kortes Dam. There is no public access available to the east side of the reservoir. Watch for golden eagles who have nests that are visible by boat on the south arm of the reservoir.

Park headquarters is located in the North Red Hills area. The Morgan Creek Big Game Winter Range is nearby where bighorn, elk and antelope winter.

INFORMATION -
Seminoe State Park
Seminoe Dam Route
Sinclair, Wyoming 82334
307-328-0115

CURT GOWDY STATE PARK
6

LOCATION - Take Happy Jack Road, or Wyoming 210, west out of Cheyenne, or go east on I-80 from Laramie. The park is also accessible from the Buford interchange on I-80 between Laramie and Cheyenne in the foothills of the Laramie Mountains.

ACTIVITIES - The park is surrounded by huge granite formations and has two small reservoirs which provide excellent fishing. Granite Reservoir is better known for its water sports including fishing and waterskiing. Swimming is not permitted in the reservoir. Limited camping is available either in the trees or along the shore line. Concessions are available during the summer.

The 10K volksmarch winds its way through hilly meadows through the highlands west of Cheyenne. You'll see unusual rock formations and two reservoirs. The Crystal Reservoir is a fisherman's haven. Hikers can enjoy tramping in the nearby hills, which are also good for rockhounding.

There is a lodge with cabins in the park. Reservations are required: 307-632-7946. Bring your own bedding, cooking and eating utensils. The lodge accommodates 30.

INFORMATION -
Curt Gowdy State Park
1351 Hynds Lodge Road
Cheyenne, Wyoming 82009
307-632-7946

EDNESS KIMBALL WILKINS STATE PARK
7

LOCATION - Three miles east of Evansville and near Casper on U.S. 26/20 along the North Platte River.

ACTIVITIES - Open for day use, you can enjoy a picnic, go hiking, fishing, swimming or riding along the bicycle trails.

The almost level 10K volksmarch's route lies in the floodplain of the North Platte River, a few miles east of Casper. The trail loops through a meadow and large grove of trees before continuing along the river bank to return to its starting point.

INFORMATION -
Edness Kimball Wilkins State Park
P.O. Box 1596
Evansville, Wyoming 82636
307-577-5150

KEYHOLE STATE PARK
8

LOCATION - Eight miles north of I-90 on Pine Ridge Road between Sundance and Moorcroft. The park lies along the southeastern shore of Keyhole Reservoir, within sight of Devils Tower National Monument and on the western edge of the Black Hills.

ACTIVITIES - You can enjoy hiking, camping, touring the visitor center, boating, swimming and fishing for walleye, catfish, bass and pike. The park has a full service marina. The reservoir's 52-mile shoreline is warm and well protected, making it ideal for water sports. Food service is available. A lodge with cabins is located on Headquarters Road, adjacent to the lake.

INFORMATION -
Keyhole State Park
Inyan Kara Route
Moorcroft, Wyoming 82721
307-756-3596

SINKS CANYON STATE PARK
9

LOCATION - Take Fifth Street, Sinks Canyon Road, south out of Lander. Turn west and continue for six more miles on Wyoming 131.

ACTIVITIES - Stop at the visitor center for an overlook of the Popo Agie River which disappears into a large limestone cavern. The river reappears downstream in an area called "The Rise" where the water wells up, sometimes exploding out of the ground in the spring when the runoff is high.

Hike the one-mile nature trail by the visitor center. For a longer hike, take the 10K volksmarch which begins at the visitor center and follows the river through meadows filled with flowers. During the spring, the yellow arrowleaf balsaroot is in full bloom, and its large yellow heads seem to track with the sun.

Another 1½-mile-long River Gorge Trail goes up to a series of waterfalls and is accessible up the road beyond the Popo Agie Campground. Drive to Bruce's Picnic Ground to reach the trailhead.

Camping in Popo Agie Campground is on a first come–first served basis. It has 25 sites, some along the roaring water of the river. Another one-mile nature trail begins from the upper end of this campground. After crossing the swinging bridge, take the trail to the left. The trail that goes up the hill in front of you is part of the volksmarch.

Rodeo fans have the opportunity to watch competitive riders and ropers do their stuff in Lander on Wednesday nights during the summer. Lander's biggest and possibly the world's oldest paid rodeo, is held on July 4th at the Lander Old Timers' Rodeo Arena. This event also features Indian relay racing.

INFORMATION -
Sinks Canyon State Park
3079 Sinks Canyon Road
Route #63
Lander, Wyoming 82520
307-332-6333

BOYSEN STATE PARK
10

LOCATION - On U.S. 20, drive 10 miles north of Shoshoni on U.S. 20 to reach the east shore of the Boysen Reservoir, or six miles west on U.S. 26, then five more miles north on the access road to reach the west shore. The park is in Wind River Canyon.

ACTIVITIES - Camp in one of eleven campgrounds that surround the reservoir or stay in a cabin below the dam at the mouth of the Wind River Canyon. The reservoir has a 76-mile shoreline where you can enjoy water sports and swimming from the beach on the east shore.

The park has a marina with a restaurant, boat rentals, fishing licenses, and a motel and cabins located on the southeast end of the reservoir. You can go fishing either in the reservoir or in the river for rainbow and brown trout, western sauger, bass, crappie and yellow perch. The volksmarch begins at the Boysen Marina.

INFORMATION -
Boysen State Park
Boysen Route
Shoshoni, Wyoming 82649
307-876-2796

BIG SANDY RECREATION AREA
11

LOCATION - Eight miles north of Farson on U.S. 191.

ACTIVITIES - Some of the best rock hunting in the state is done here along with water sports along its 17-mile shoreline. Go fishing for cutthroat, rainbow and brown trout and catfish.

INFORMATION -
Big Sandy Recreation Area
307-876-2796

State Park Index

KEY TO THE INDEX

CG = Campground FS = Fishing HK = Hiking CO = Concessions
VC = Visitor's Center WA = Water Activities PG = Page

Park Name	CG	FS	HK	CO	VC	WA	PG

ALASKA

Park Name	CG	FS	HK	CO	VC	WA	PG
Captain Cook	●	●	●			●	7
Chatanika River	●	●				●	8
Chena River	●	●	●			●	8
Chilkat	●	●	●			●	9
Chugach	●	●	●				9
Denali	●	●	●		●	●	10
Fort Ambercrombie	●		●		●		12
Independence Mine				●			13
Kepler-Bradley Lakes	●	●					13
Nancy Lake	●	●	●			●	14
Sitka State Parks							14
Refuge Cove		●					14
Settlers Cove	●	●	●				14
Pioneer Park				●			15
Baranof Castle							15
Totem Bight				●			15
Wichersham							16

NEVADA

NEW MEXICO

OREGON

UTAH

The Author

Vici DeHaan has been an elementary school teacher in the Boulder Valley Schools for 31 years where she has taught grades K-6. She is the author of seven other books: *Bicycling the Colorado Rockies*, *Hiking Trails of the Boulder Mountain Parks and Plains*, *Moving Through the Ratings: Passing from Private to Professional Pilot*, *The Runner's Guide to Boulder County*, *Bike Rides of the Colorado Front Range*, *Pilot's Cross-Country Guide to National Parks and Historical Monuments*, and *The Pilot's Cross-Country Guide to National Parks*.

Vici DeHaan is an avid outdoors person who has hiked in the Colorado Rockies all her life. She became involved in a running career in her 40s by first competing in the Denver Marathon. To date she has run 13 marathons including two times up and down Pikes Peak and has run the New York Marathon twice. Vici has also become involved in triathlons and has competed in 14 of them. She has held several age group records, and in 1988, was selected for the All-American Triathlon Team. To date she has competed in almost 400 races of varying lengths.

Vici holds a private pilot's license and a ground instructor's rating. She and her husband, Warren, have flown their light plane all over the United States, Canada and Mexico. They live in Boulder, Colorado, and have five children and two grandchildren.

Other Outdoor Guides from Cordillera Press

ARIZONA'S MOUNTAINS
A Hiking and Climbing Guide
Bob and Dotty Martin

COLORADO'S CONTINENTAL DIVIDE
A Hiking and Backpacking Guide
Ron Ruhoff

COLORADO'S HIGH THIRTEENERS
A Climbing and Hiking Guide
Mike Garratt and Bob Martin

MEXICO'S COPPER CANYON COUNTRY
A Hiking and Backpacking Guide to Tarahumara-land
M. John Fayhee

TAKE 'EM ALONG
Sharing the Wilderness with Your Children
Barbara J. Euser

THE OUTDOOR ATHLETE
Total Training for Outdoor Performance
Steve Ilg

THE SAN JUAN MOUNTAINS
A Climbing and Hiking Guide
Robert F. Rosebrough

2591